May this book bring you
insight & peace

Frank & Dorothy

Frank J. Steffler & Dorothy J. Steffler

ISBN: 978-1-77069-563-4

Printed in Canada

Word Alive Press
131 Cordite Road, Winnipeg, MB R3W 1S1
www.wordalivepress.ca

Library and Archives Canada Cataloguing in Publication

Steffler, Frank J. (Frank James), 1951-

Nurturing your hidden spirit : straight talk about spiritual & psychological development / Frank J. Steffler & Dorothy J. Steffler.

ISBN 978-1-77069-563-4

1. Self-realization. 2. Spirituality--Psychology. 3. Spiritual life. I. Steffler, Dorothy J. (Dorothy Jane), 1953- II. Title.

BF637.S4S74 2012 158.1 C2012-903100-3

dedication

To our three girls, our great sons-in-law,
and our beautiful grandchildren.
May you be inspired to nurture your hidden spirit.

acknowledgements

Thank you to all who shared your stories and comments in helping form this book, especially to Father Ubald Duchesneau, OMI, whose biblical wisdom is an ever-freeing message for all people.

table of contents

preface

I stood among the rows of cold, stately tombstones. The grave was fresh with a freshly raked mound of earth yet to be sodded and yet to take on that well-manicured look symbolizing the closure on grief that accompanies the loss of a dear friend. I stared at the elaborate floral sprays only slightly wilted since yesterday's service. I reflected on the last moments I'd shared with my good friend, just being with him at his bedside as he waited for the cancer to release him to his own glorious resurrection. I had studied under my mentor for six, seven, maybe even eight years—the number didn't matter. What mattered was that this humble man had changed my life in ways that could never be imagined.

Near the east end of the graveyard, I sauntered toward the weathered monument of dear Brother Anthony. On the base, the inscription read "Expect Miracles" in sharp contrast to what I remember my Father Ubald saying so often: "There are no miracles." How could two holy men, saints in my eyes but definitely mystics—both having a special relationship with God—have such blatantly opposite views of what God was about? One says to expect miracles; the other, there are no miracles. How could it be? What is the truth? Questions, always questions, always searching, struggling, bewildered, frustrated, angry, hurt… I know now that I must share my journey, knowing there are no answers but love, and no questions for which love is not the answer.

—Frank Steffler

THE HUMAN *Experience*

chapter one

We write this book from the perspective that it is possible for a human being to actually experience glimpses of God. In fact, if you look at the psychological literature, there is little doubt that experiencing the transcendent—a certain "oneness" or "otherness"—is a genuine human experience.

How people describe this experience differs greatly. Some say they experience God through nature, some through intellectual enlightenment, some through a relationship, and others following an experience of love, death, or loss. Some of us have such a profound personal experience of God that it changes us forever. We have what is sometimes called a "St. Paul" experience—a conversion. St. Francis, one of the great saints of the Catholic Church, had such an experience while recovering from near-fatal war wounds during the Crusades. When he came home from war, he embraced a new life of love and service to the poor. He literally shed all his worldly belongings, of which he had many, and gave everything to the poor. His conversion was so profound that he became the founder of one of the most well-known and largest religious communities, the Franciscan Friars, Poor Clare Order of nuns, and Secular Franciscan Order of laity. We are professed members of the Secular Franciscan Order.

Because everyone's experience of God is different and so deeply personal, is it any wonder that people, at least ordinary people like us, have a difficult time expressing our experience and sharing it with others? Yet if we could only let down our own defences, or just have the right words to express ourselves, these experiences are probably what we would most want to share with those we care about.

Our goal in this book is to share some of our

own encounters with the sacred, with our God. We will attempt to integrate these experiences with what is written in the sacred Christian scriptures and the social sciences literature. Our hope is that our stories will encourage you to become seekers of your own God and to live a fulfilling and meaningful life with and for those you love.

So, whether you're at ease talking about your relationship with God or not—or perhaps you doubt that you've ever experienced God, that it is even possible, or you feel uncomfortable talking about your deeply personal experiences—we are writing this book for you. We hope that our stories will resonate with your stories and that you will agree that there's nothing more valuable than becoming aware of how our God is active in our lives.

The literature tells us that faith and spirituality are developmental, and most often begin when we are young (Cox, 2005; Fowler, 1981, 1996). According to Fowler, faith development is inextricably dependent on biological maturation, emotional and cognitive development, psychosocial experience, and cultural influences. When we say something is developmental, we mean that it's dynamic and ever-changing. There's nothing static about our understanding of God or our own spirituality. James Fowler is best known for his research and description of faith development, which he describes as progressing through seven stages, which begin in infancy.

Stage 0: Primal Faith. This stage begins in the first year of a child's life, before the infant can even speak. The development of faith begins with mutual interaction between the infant and the primary caregiver. The infant begins to develop the foundation of trust versus mistrust, the first stage in Erikson's psychosocial stages of development (Erikson, 1968). The type of experiences that lead to this sense of trust are commonplace for infants with attentive, caring parents, the type of care that psychologists say leads to a healthy and secure parent-child attachment. Infants are thrust into this unpredictable world completely dependent on others to care for their basic needs and comfort. Infants learn to trust the world when they have caregivers who provide trusting bodily contact, who nourish, talk, and play with their infants, and who are attentive to overstimulation and generally in tune with the child's needs (Fowler, 1996). Loving, consistent care in infancy provides the foundation for faith development in adulthood.

Stage 1: Intuitive-Projective Faith. This very early stage of faith is built upon the child's imaginative view of the world. In very early childhood, faith is stimulated by stories, gestures, and symbols. God is perceived as powerful and can do anything, much like Superman and Santa Claus (Fowler, 1996). Fowler calls this the impulsive self.

Stage 2: Mythic-Literal Faith. As logical thinking develops, children are able to view the world from others' perspectives. They begin to think of the world in concrete forms, unlike the intuitive, imaginative thinking of the previous stage. Their logic is based on cause-and-effect experiences, an understanding of space and time. Piaget (1970) calls this period of development concrete operational thought. Children are able to make inferences about another's behaviour and perceived intentions; justice is concrete, reciprocal, and fair (Parker, 2006). The world is perceived as orderly and predictable, black and white. Ambiguities aren't considered. Children are comforted by the security of parental authority. This is a crucial stage for all forms of development, including faith development. This predictability, logical cause and effect, and black-and-white, justice-oriented morality provide the foundation for further growth and new forms of knowledge in later development. Fowler calls this the imperial self.

Stage 3: Synthetic-Conventional Faith. Normal cognitive development moves from concrete thinking to the ability to think abstractly. Piaget calls this formal operational thought and it generally emerges in adolescence and continues to develop throughout the lifespan. This is the same time that adolescents struggle with forming their personal identity (Erikson, 1968). Part of this abstract thinking is the ability to integrate multiple self-concepts into a coherent self-identity. Faith identity is part of this process. Identity formation is a gradual process that builds on interpersonal relationships and experiences. At this stage, one's faith identity is based on the values and beliefs of others. Although one's belief system is relatively unexamined at this stage, it may be deeply felt. God takes on the qualities of a good friend (Parker, 2006). Fowler calls this the interpersonal self.

Stage 4: Individuative-Reflective Faith. This stage emerges as a result of intentional reflection on one's beliefs and faith. It requires the ability to look at one's belief system from an objective, third-party perspective, which includes oneself, others, and a social system (Fowler, 1996). It requires an understanding of how a person's actions impact others as well as society in general. People in this stage often go through a critical examination of their previously held beliefs and attempt to reconcile contradictions and inconsistencies. For some, this may result in estrangement from previously valued faith groups (Parker, 2006). For others, it may result in recommitment to the broader institutionally sanctioned belief system. Societal institutions may provide a means of expressing one's identity. Regardless, meaning is found in being part of something beyond oneself and others. Through this internalization of authority, people are able to make commitments to an ideology and lifestyle (Fowler, 1996). God is truth, justice, and love (Parker, 2006). Fowler calls this the institutional self.

Stage 5: Conjunctive Faith. In mid-life, people often go through a period of reflection on what they've missed in life. With faith issues, this might mean revisiting the inconsistencies that were previously thought to be reconciled. This period of life often brings with it a desire to bring together what appear to be paradoxical realities and polarities. It may involve examining other traditions, other cultures. In the search for ultimate meaning, one feels a desire for social inclusiveness. God includes mystery and paradox (Parker, 2006). Fowler calls this the interindividual self.

Stage 6: Universalizing Faith. Following mid-life, Fowler suggests people move to a universalized faith that encompasses all that is good, a oneness with life, with being. This transcendence is grounded in personal beliefs and a commitment to universal values of freedom, justice, dignity, and love.

* * *

As children, our faith is simple and based on what our parents, or others in authority, have told us. This is Fowler's "literal faith" stage. Most of us are taught to believe that we experience God through church, prayer, relationships, nature, and perhaps even animals, pets, gifts, or events. Throughout this book, we will use some of our own personal experiences and draw from a wide variety of religious and spiritual experiences so generously shared by other people as illustrations of how God actively works in our lives through ordinary and sometimes extraordinary events.

* * *

Frank: In the summer of my ninth birthday, I moved from the city to a small Mennonite hamlet of less than a hundred people. Many were poor and backward, according to today's standards. But this is where I grew up. My dad bought me a pony named Toby. I'd chase my sister around the big yard, and one day I accidentally killed her cat with a stone. I didn't have the courage to tell her the truth until I was well past my fortieth birthday!

My dad had a small fruit and vegetable farm to supplement his income from the meatpacking plant, a respectable job he held for more than forty years. He kept me busy mowing the lawn, weeding the gardens, and picking endless strawberries and raspberries. My family lived by a meandering river that highlighted the changing seasons and provided a habitat for various animals, all lovely to watch, and peaceful. I fished weekly and the family ate all the fish we could debone.

The two-room school I attended was rough and tough. A coal furnace kept us dirty, warm, and smelly in the winter—and dirty, warm, and smelly in the summer. The school's windows were a perfect target for knocking baseballs through. Leaf-houses and football games were especially fun. With exciting Christmas concerts, planning parties after church, and winning county baseball championships, most aspects of my life were quite rewarding. This is also where I learned about the birds and the bees; boobs were soft, and homemade wine gave you a severe headache. But some things were better left unsaid. I remember telling everyone that my aunt was pregnant—and received the strap for using such coarse language. My parents had been excited about my aunt's most recent baby, so I'd thought it would be good news! Enough said.

Sometime during my early elementary school years, the priest told all the families in the church that it was important for their children to have religion taught to them by a nun. From then on, for two weeks every summer, I dutifully attended. As a young boy, you can picture me bicycling to the local church for an hour along a gravel road on a hot summer's day, my Lone Ranger lunchbox tied to the back of my bike. Here, I experienced summer catechism classes in an old church hall. There were long tables where the nuns "from the city" drilled us with the right answers to the catechism questions, taught us prayers and religious songs, worked on crafts, and played games. These black-and-white nuns were very mysterious in their tightly coiffed veils and starched wimples.

I also learned about God through institutional religious processes, all of which provided a template for one to be a *good person*. I learned about what is good, what is bad, and what we must do to get to heaven. It was during one of these weeks that I built a little altar in my bedroom. I prayed dutifully, morning and night. One night, I had a dream about a man in a brown robe walking along a narrow path. I tried calling to him; he turned but kept on walking, as if summoning me to follow. It didn't mean anything to me at the time. Later, I became a Franciscan and dedicated my life to the way of St. Francis, whose hallmark was a brown robe. Imagine that!

* * *

Many of us learned formal ways to pray, either in formal settings like Frank's or from our parents or other family members. Whatever our tradition and culture, we pass on a sense of our traditional religious behaviour to the next generation. This is a beginning, or as Fowler would say, "mythic-literal faith."

Many say that faith is caught and not taught. This implies that what we see and experience in our upbringing determines our own faith experience. Children most often imitate those who are important to them—their parents, siblings, and close friends—and they're most likely to imitate what is highly valued and acceptable (Bandura, 1977).

So yes, in this sense, faith is caught. But that's not the whole story. Faith development is a combination of human influence, cognitive decision, and God's Spirit continuously prompting us, encouraging our openness and response. Without the influence of God's Spirit in our lives, we would merely be conditioned to behave in a manner similar to what we see in others, a mere imitation of religiosity. The Spirit, however, is forever calling us to meaningfulness, to an otherness, something that mere imitation of external behaviour cannot accomplish. This prompting, encouraging, and calling from God all occurs within a normal journey of life, packed with human interactions with others and typical human experiences.

How does this Spirit call us and encourage us? God works through the laws of nature. The action of the Spirit in our lives parallels the seasons of life that occur through natural human development—from infancy, early childhood, adolescence, and young and middle adulthood on to old age. Our spiritual life isn't separate from our biological, psychological, and sociological reality. We aren't compartmentalized; we are whole human beings. Each aspect of our existence influences the whole person. The dynamic situations of change and growth in our lives stir opportunities for us to develop deeper personal relationships with our God and, consequently, become more fully alive ourselves. The Spirit invites the god of imitation to become a real and personal God—our God. *My* God. These opportunities are presented to each of us, constantly, for *"there is no favouritism with God"* Galatians 2:6 (NJB). How we respond to these opportunities as human beings serves us either well or not so well. God has created us with intellect and free will, the two things that separate us from all other living things. Out of this knowledge and freedom to choose, we create our journey and purpose in life.

In researching faith stories for this book, a colleague told me of a faith experience from his youth. When he was a young boy, he went on a holiday and decided to try surfing off the West Coast. A huge wave came in, took him under, and a little while later he ended up floating and stunned too far from shore, his body exhausted. There was nobody around. How would he survive? Suddenly, a fellow appeared with two surfboards. He gave the young boy one of his boards, saying, "Here, take this and head for shore," then paddled off. The young boy looked back and saw no one, dismayed and awed as he finally reached the shore (Daniel Becker, personal communication).

My colleague is now a mature middle-age man in the construction industry, but he remembers and retells the story as an encounter with someone or something from God—an angel, a guide, but definitely from God. He tells me the story with all the vivid details, and still after all these years he has that same sense of awe for what happened. When he told me the story, he hesitated to say what or who this person was who essentially saved his life. Could it be that he had an experience of the Divine, where God, through the Spirit, mixed with natural law and brought this young boy to safety?

As scripture says in the book of Wisdom,

> *Yes, Lord, in every way you have made your people great and glorious; you have never failed*

to help them at any time or place. (Wisdom 19:22, NJB)

I do believe, help my unbelief! (Mark 9:24, NAB)

* * *

Frank: I had a similar experience. When I was sixteen years old, I decided I was man enough to explore the country. I took the train across Canada, from my small home town in southern Ontario to Vancouver. I wanted to see the world. I was walking along the shoreline in Stanley Park, lost in my own thoughts and dreams of the future, when a man seemed to appear out of nowhere.

"Get out of here!" he said eagerly. "You have to get out of here, now! The tide's coming in and you won't make it back to shore. There's a walkway right here. Just go right up."

I had no experience of the ocean, but I heard the urgency in his voice. Fearing what I knew nothing about, I scurried back to the trail and began the upward climb. Then it dawned on me that the man wasn't following me. I looked back and thought, *Holy cats! Look at that tide coming in. I could have drowned!* I looked for the man and he was nowhere to be seen, yet I clearly remember the man had continued walking out toward the tide. There was no other path leading away from the ocean other than the trail he had pointed me to. I found out later that the tide in that area was upwards of twenty feet. I would have surely drowned without this warning. But where had the man gone?

* * *

These stories don't just come from young people. A salesman named Ben in a remote northern area of Alberta told us of yet another life-changing experience. One bleak wintery day, he was driving along Highway 43 toward Grande Prairie when he checked his rear-view mirror and noticed a large semi-tractor trailer coming up fast behind him. He shortly passed over the crest of a hill only to see in front of him an old boat of a car turning into his lane. To make matters worse, a van was approaching in the opposite lane and the road was covered in a sheet of solid ice. He had nowhere to go!

In a split second, Ben thought, *Hit the ditch!* But instantly the van in the opposing lane veered over to the shoulder, creating enough room for Ben to sneak right through the centre. Zoom… unbelievable! Ben said the close call took a couple of years off his life, but he believed it was only through the grace of God that he was still alive today (Ben Dyck, personal communication).

When we began our research for this book, we talked to many men and women, young and old. Most were very private about their ideas of God. A large percentage hesitated to share what they truly felt and believed. However, a number were happy to share these stories—leaving the conclusions up to the listener.

We could speculate about what these stories mean. Was God, through the Spirit, physically present? Are these angel stories? What could make us think these everyday occurrences happened through the grace of God? Could it be the prompting and calling of the Spirit, or is it only the actions of human beings that seem, somehow, to be there for us at the right time and place to save, or at least change, our lives? According to psychological literature, such experiences occur to people both within and outside established religious traditions. The experiences seem to have the same underlying theme, regardless of the source or the interpretation (Hood, 1977). The theme is generally awe-inspiring, unforgettable, and often unexplainable.

Being touched by God, however this happens, is mystical. To be mystical is to have a spiritual meaning. The word mystical is defined in Webster's dictionary as:

> (a) having a spiritual meaning or reality that is neither apparent to the senses nor obvious to the intelligence, (b) involving or having the nature of an individual's direct subjective communion with God or ultimate reality—the mystical food of the sacrament—the mystical

> experience of the Inner Light—the mystical experience of the Awe of God through a life experience, with another person, with nature, with intuition. (Webster, p. 785)

Clearly all those who told us their stories felt a sense of awe and couldn't explain their experiences through natural law and intelligence. Thalbourne (2003) says a mystical experience is:

> An experience which... consists of a majority of the following features: it tends to be sudden in onset, joyful, and difficult to verbalize; it involves a sense of perceiving the purpose of existence; an insight into "the harmony of things"; a perception of an ultimate unity—of oneness; transcendence of the ego; an utter conviction of immortality; and it tends to be temporary, authoritative and attributed supreme value. Some people interpret the mystical experience as an experience of unity with God. (pp. 74–75)

So, were these experiences mystical? I'll leave that for you to decide.

FAITH BUILDS ON *Nature*

chapter two

Dorothy: These unexplainable experiences are intriguing, for sure. They heighten our awareness of the spiritual side of life, but these are not the bricks and mortar of our faith development and spiritual identity. Our faith develops from the people who have influenced our spirituality. Our parents, teachers, relatives, partners, children, siblings, and even strangers initiate and profoundly impact how we see God.

When I think back to my childhood faith experiences, I was immersed in traditional Catholic family life. I went to a Catholic elementary school, church on Sundays and holy days (days set aside by the church to especially remember important saints), strawberry socials in the summer, and piano lessons at the convent. One of my fondest childhood memories was the day I made my First Holy Communion. It was a breezy Sunday morning in June. I wore the same white communion dress that my four sisters had worn before me. It was the most beautiful dress I had ever seen. I remember feeling so special, and a bit self-conscious, because the size of my hoop crinoline made the skirt really big and a little too short. Mom made a beautiful lily-of-the-valley tiara from the dainty flowers that grew so prolifically in the north flowerbed of our farm home. To this day, those flowers remind me of my first Communion Day. The white veil fell just to my elbows. I had brand new white patent-leather shoes for the occasion. My godparents and grandparents came for the special event and we had a big Sunday dinner to celebrate. I was princess for the day!

* * *

These simple, seemingly "old world" church experiences during our upbringings have a profound influence on our images of God and how we respond to religion for the rest of our lives. These early institutional experiences provide a foundation, a benchmark, something to begin with and build on. Those who study religion and psychology often describe religion as a two-sided experience: cultural and personal (Corveleyn & Luyten, 2005). In this sense, our early church experiences provide us with the cultural symbols that motivate us to develop a personal religion.

What if we don't have these early traditional church experiences? Recent polls suggest that 94% of Americans (Nierenberg & Sheldon, 2005) and 72% of Canadians (Avery, 2008) believe in God, although only about one-third attend church at least once a month (Statistics Canada, 2006). Scripture says that God has no favourites. Our ideas about religion, and particularly about God, come from many sources, including the influence of significant others in our lives, in interaction with our social and cultural environment (Rizzuto, 1979). Yes, our early experiences of attending church are tremendously important, but so, too, are other, perhaps less salient experiences. God works through our natural environment. Often our ideas about God surface when there's a crisis in our lives or when we have a major decision to make.

Regardless of whether or not one has had a traditional church upbringing, the search for the sacred is a common human experience. Some would say the search for the sacred within the context of traditional church or communal beliefs is *religious*, whereas the search for the sacred within one's personal experiences is *spirituality* (Zinnbauer & Pargament, 2005).

These two constructs are complex and multifaceted. It is not our purpose to explain or defend the various definitions. That endeavour would be distracting and lose relevance. It is sufficient to underline the fact that searching for the sacred is a common human experience. People are motivated to look for and hold on to that which they find meaningful and significant in their lives. Sometimes what they find and try to hold on to leads to change and transformation (Zinnbauer & Pargament, 2005). Again, we see a developmental theme. Our ideas about the sacred, religion, and spirituality are constantly changing, thus faith develops within the context of our everyday life experiences. Faith builds on human nature.

In the first chapter, we mentioned Fowler's stages of faith development, which are linked to cognitive development, moving from the concrete to the abstract. Fowler's approach works well in describing faith development from childhood to adulthood. There are other ways of framing the development of our faith, however. Oser and Gmünder (Oser, 1991; Oser & Gmünder, 1991), for example, present a series of stages that describe patterns of religious judgements based on solutions to real-life situations that describe one's perception of how God interacts with humans in different circumstances, such as when there's a tragedy or an important decision to make. One stage isn't better than another, merely different, depending on how we understand God in a particular situation. These five stages can be summarized as follows:

Stage 1. Divine intervention influences and produces unexpected and unsolicited effects in our day-to-day lives. God is seen as active in the world and people simply react to God's actions. In this stage, people unabatedly believe the world unfolds according to God's design and our role is to respond in good faith. A young couple tries for many years to conceive a child and eventually concedes, "It must be God's will that we don't have a child." God has a plan, but that plan is separate from ours. God isn't acting with us, but upon us. The image of God is as a watchmaker. It's as if the events of our lives are predestined.

Stage 2. The individual influences Divine intervention through prayer and good/bad deeds. We make promises to God. We bargain with God. A drunk driver prays that if God will only see him home safely, he will never drink again. How often do we say, "Please God, get me through this; I won't ever do it again"? This stage is reminiscent of the verse from Maria and the Captain's song in the musical *The Sound of Music*: "So here you are standing there loving me, whether or not you should... Somewhere in my wicked, miserable past, I must have done something good" (Rodgers, 1964). In this stage, we believe God rewards us when we've been good. And when bad things happen, we believe we are being punished. God is a judging God. We interpret both worldly and personal events to mean God is happy or unhappy with us. I won the lottery; God must be happy with me. There's an outbreak of AIDS in the world; God is punishing us for our horrible sins.

Stage 3. The Divine withdraws and the individual is responsible for him or herself. This is the opposite of the first stage. In this stage, it is typical for people to believe that God simply doesn't answer prayers. A young mother loses her child to cancer. She has been pleading desperately for a cure… with no answer. A child is lost at a family picnic in the park and never found—or worse yet, only a body is found. How can an active, loving God allow such horrific events to occur? At first glance, one might think this stage is a regression of faith. In fact, it is developmental, because people in this stage are able to make the distinction between God's existence outside of the created world (the transcendent God) and within the created world (the immanent God) (Oser, 1991). In some traditions, there is a belief that this world is created as a testing ground to see if one is "good enough" to abide with the All-Powerful and Mighty God for eternity.

Stage 4. The Divine is relative to one's own perception. At this stage, people realize that there are limits to one's own autonomy as it is the Divine who gives meaning to life (Oser, 1991). However, the

Divine is different for everyone, just as the way one finds meaning is unique to each individual. There is a sense of freedom at this stage—freedom to create one's own perception of God, which is often experienced as a walk through nature, the stillness of a babbling brook, or the miracle of life when a baby is born. One has a perception that there's something outside oneself that is beautiful and transcendent—an awe experience.

Stage 5. The Divine is somehow united with the individual. The individual is free to make autonomous decisions but sees him or herself as connected to the Divine. People in this stage are generally drawn to serve their fellow human beings through love and care. Mother Teresa exemplified this stage of faith in her ultimate care and love for the poorest of the poor who lay dying in the gutters of Calcutta. St. Francis of Assisi embraced and cared for lepers, the outcasts of society. Oser calls this "universal and unconditional religiosity" (Oser, 1991, p. 10). In this stage, our free will is not about *my will* but rather *Thy will.* St. Augustine of Hippo (c. 400 AD) framed this concept of freedom well with his words "love God and do what you will." He was encouraging people to love God to such an extent that they would only want to love others as God loves. All Christians have been called to such love:

> *Jesus said…* "You must love the Lord your God with all your heart, with all your soul,

> and with all your mind. *This is the greatest and the first commandment. The second resembles it:* You must love your neighbour as yourself." (Matthew 22:37–39, NJB, emphasis added)

In the earlier stages of faith development, people have a tendency to see God's actions in the world in extremes—either God is active or not, God hears my prayers or does not, God rewards or punishes. In later stages, people have the ability to integrate such polarities—"I have free will, but I can also count on God to help me make good decisions." God is transcendent and immanent at once.

Oser (1991), similar to developmental psychologists in other areas, suggests that movement from one stage to the next occurs when we encounter a problem or difficulty in our lives that our current way of thinking cannot resolve. So what pushes us forward? Our current way of approaching life just doesn't work. We have a crisis in our lives and we search for a solution. Is this the Spirit of God working through hardships to bring us closer to the unity that Oser describes, or is it simply human nature? If it's human nature, what (or Who) determined that humans should respond in such a fashion?

THE SEARCH–*Man*

chapter three

Frank: I managed to memorize all five pages of questions and answers for my Confirmation, except I didn't give a totally correct answer when the Bishop quizzed me. But hopefully the Holy Spirit came anyway. Thus, after some fights, some pain, and not much gain, I left high school for a trade, thanks to my great uncle (and godfather) who built about fifty custom homes a year. He was a well-respected building contractor and was willing to take me on as an apprentice. Being a tradesman seemed to fit for me, and the opportunity was there. Talk about the influence of a few major people in a person's life!

While still in my very young and impressionable years, I met another survivor who was looking for excitement and purpose in life. We got married and left home as high school sweethearts. That's what you did in those days. There were no children for our first seven years, so we partied hard and had many a cold meal because passion couldn't wait.

Eventually, with much study, a few good people, and a good economy, I became a superintendent, project manager, and then built some impressive construction projects, along with my first new home—all by the ripe age of twenty-one. By twenty-six, I had my own contracting company. Life was good.

My religious experiences were part of the good, although at this time they were very much habit-driven. We went to church every Sunday even though I remember feeling like I could hardly wait until it was over so I could go home and get on with my day. I did pretend I was pure and holy a few times, by giving up drinking and smoking for Lent, which does have a way of making Easter one hell of a celebration.

Two children later, around the time of our tenth wedding anniversary, Ontario went into a recession.

What did I do? I had just built my second new home, I had two children, and my wife wasn't working. Desperate times call for desperate measures! One of those black-and-white nuns told me about special prayers called novenas. They were sure to work, especially if you prayed to the big saints. If you promised to say the same prayer for nine days, your prayers would definitely be answered. I rummaged through my shoebox of keepsakes and dug out one of my old childhood prayer books, relieved to find a novena to St. Theresa.

So, on the ninth day, I flew out to Edmonton, Alberta, to have a look around. They called it "Boomtown" back then. Somehow, on that first night, twenty-five hundred miles from home, alone, on the seventh floor of the Holiday Inn, something happened. The only explanation I've ever had for it is that I had a conversion of some sort—I was touched by God. A spiritual conversion is really a turning back, a calling back to something deeper, something more meaningful than what we are living at the time.

I think my conversion was the result of fear and being in a strange place, away from home and worried about the responsibility before me. God works through natural law. This crisis brought me to my knees. Fortunately, God responded immediately. I knelt down at the bed, crying, "What am I doing here?" I prayed for God to look after me. I promised that if everything worked out, I'd pray more. I'd go to church once a week on a regular basis. I'd be a good person. I promised! All I asked was that he see me through this crisis. What a perfect example of Oser's (1991) stage-two faith. I bargained with God, made promises, and hoped that if I was good enough, God would answer my prayers.

I got up the next day and landed both a great job and a great place to live. Was that Divine providence or luck? I was twenty-nine. It was at this specific time that my life began to diverge in two distinct directions and successes: one, a successful career in construction; and two, twelve years of formal theological studies. Dealing with these two paths created a great deal of tension and confusion in my life. Eventually, I felt I had to make a choice between them.

I chose what I thought was the "higher" road. I spent a good number of years doing pastoral work in parishes, prisons, hospitals, and on the street working with many cultural groups. These were good times. I learned a lot about life, about death, about struggle, and about celebration. I learned about growth and positive disintegration—the struggle and pain one experiences before growth and new life can take hold.

> *Unless a wheat grain falls into the earth and dies, it remains only a single grain.* (John 12:24, NJB)

Much later, my thinking changed. Spurred by these experiences, along with many discussions that caused the reflection and impetus for this book, I realized these divergent paths were actually one and the same path. Lots of stories came to light over the years of the working man and his God—like the man who was pouring a fifty-thousand-dollar concrete slab when it began to rain all around him, except on the slab (Ted Kotylak, personal communication). I've personally heard at least three of these exact stories, including one just the other day. What is it about God and the weather? Coincidental—or providential?

There were other stories of encounters with God—such as a person detecting the fragrance of roses when there were no rose bushes in sight, near-misses of workers getting hurt on construction sites, and the perfect job coming up for a person at the perfect time. These stories were always told with a sense of awe and wonder. They always left me pondering what great cosmic order created these natural miracles/awe experiences.

A good professor of mine used the Latin phrase *dabitur vobis*, meaning "it will be given to you," referring to Jesus' response to his disciples upon their return after he initially sent them out to minister and they responded, in exhaustion, "We don't know what to say to people when they ask us questions." Jesus answered, "Don't worry about what you're to say, as it will be given to you by the Spirit. Just tell the people what you've seen and how you've experienced the love of God." And so we see that the power of our words comes from our experiences and the convictions of our heart.

Men are concrete. The search for God is manifest in real-life experience.

A great holy man once told me that the surest sign of the presence of God in a person's life is the three R's: "The *right* person in the *right* place at the *right* time." These three R's have been proven by many men's stories about having experienced the presence of God periodically throughout their lives.

Over the years, I've had many discussions with men about their belief systems. I believe the same discussions prevail in all men all over the world, but few have the openness or opportunity to develop their yearnings for God without proper guidance. Many men say that religion is foremost in their thoughts—not government, culture, or society's values and prioritized norms. These material things that seemingly, and unfortunately, most often direct and dictate our lives aren't foremost in men's thoughts when they're given the chance, and the ear, to be heard.

Men are concrete. They look for God in the physical. If God is love, then I know how love works for me. For men, love is often equated with sexuality. Men equate the vulnerability of their humanity and physiology with the drive to procreate—their sexuality—which often leads to a sense of guilt. So, the physiological trap hampers their search and leads them back to self rather than otherness. They lose sight of the transcendent because their humanity gets in the way. They give up searching.

THE SEARCH

-Woman

c h a p t e r f o u r

Dorothy: All I ever wanted was to have a family. I prayed for a child… and waited… and waited. Finally, after seven years of marriage, my husband and I were blessed with a daughter. She was nine months old, the most beautiful, delicate little girl you could imagine. I didn't know anything about being a mother; thank goodness she was (and is) resilient. Before long, there was another, and then another. My life was full. I was content… at least, when my husband was content. It seemed an impossible sacrifice to move away from my family in Ontario to Alberta. All those I knew who'd done such a thing never came back! But our novena was answered, so move is what we did.

I didn't make promises. I didn't see God in changing weather patterns or providing the perfect job at the perfect time. But I knew God was in charge. I just felt it. I had made new friends at the church we attended. These friends seemed closer to me than any I had ever known. We prayed together, read spiritual books together, and compared our spiritual journeys to the holy women and men we read about. We shared on a level that I never knew existed. We had a spiritual bond, a sisterhood that filled me with a sense of meaning and profound love. I had experiences of the presence of God in ways that I had never believed possible.

> *The days are coming, the Lord declares, when I will make a new covenant with the House of Israel… when those days have come, the Lord declares: In their minds I shall plant my laws writing them on their hearts. Then I shall be their God, and they shall be my people.* (Hebrews 8:8, 10, NJB)

Women are relational. The search for God is manifest in real-life relationships.

It isn't a surprise that women talk about their relationship with God. Women talk about all their relationships. It's what we do. It also isn't a surprise that women become involved in church life. The pews are filled with women. They look for God in the relational. If God is love, then I know how love works for me.

For women, love is often equated with emotions, but sometimes women become addicted to the emotional highs. The psychological trap hampers their search and leads back to self, rather than otherness. They lose sight of the transcendent because their emotions get in the way. They confuse themselves by blurring the psychological, emotional reward often found in fantasy with the authenticity of the Divine.

> *So God created humankind in his image, in the image of God he created them; male and female he created them.* (Genesis 1:27, NRSV)

God, who has created thousands and thousands of different species, all different, and with a unique purpose, has also created each one of us unique and with our own purpose. Each one of us has our own time with our God. God will reach out to us and, with ultimate patience, wait for our response. To think there's only one path to God is to limit God and deny that we all contribute as co-creators in the universe of life. Our vocation is to share fully in Jesus' becoming fully the Son of God. We share more fully each day through the Spirit in God's Cosmic Mystery, the same fullness of Being that Jesus became at the Resurrection. This is the whole context of our spirituality. What belongs to God belongs to us, co-heirs with Jesus.

> *For all who are led by the Spirit of God* are *children of God.* (Romans 8:14, NRSV, emphasis added)

> *And if children, then heirs of God and joint heirs with Christ—if, in fact, we suffer with him so that we may also be glorified with him.* (Romans 8:17, NRSV)

> *And we bring you the good news that what God promised to our ancestors he has fulfilled for us, their children, by raising Jesus; as also it is written in the second psalm, "You are my Son; today I have begotten you."* (Acts 13:32–33, NRSV)

God's first thought was to create people who would become what God's Son Jesus would become when Jesus became human. God's goal was that we all share the Godly peace and joy of sharing and fully enjoying the happiness of creation.

> It is natural that each person should love that which he is like. Therefore, God created you to his image and likeness so that you might love him and your neighbour. (Johann Arndt, 1606)

It is our spiritual side that gives us freedom, guidance, and assures us that it's okay to be *ourselves*, to have self-affection for who we are, as we are. Ordinary men and women need to be able to think and interpret God's Spirit on their own, in their own time, building a relationship with God through their own conscience. But we need to be guided, because we often do feel lost in our day-to-day spiritual lives (Maurizio Iaccino, personal communication). We need someone to say, "You're doing everything right, you're okay," without judgement. God is essentially saying to us, "I simply love you the way you are because that's the way I made you, and it's all good. You are all good."

> *In the image of God he created them… God saw everything that he had made, and indeed, it was very good.* (Genesis 1:27, 31, NRSV)

THE IMAGE OF *God*

chapter five

There was once a little girl who told her minister that she wished God was like her father. When the minister asked her why, the little girl responded, "Because Daddy loves me and always forgives me, even if I do something wrong. I'm afraid God will lock me in the cellar if he ever finds out what I've done."

Her daddy always went the extra mile in caring for her, offering her a life experience of peacefulness and forgiving love. Unfortunately, from what she had heard about God, she felt she was doomed to be punished for everything she ever did wrong. Unlike her loving human father, this little girl's image of God as father was threatening and foreboding (Ubald Duchesneau, personal communication).

We can understand, on a purely logical and human level, why a father would be kind and forgiving of his young, innocent daughter. Only a warped, sick, and extremely broken person wouldn't relate to one's own child in such a way. How is it that we can't see our Father/Mother God in at least as loving a manner? We say God is loving, but we worry that if we break God's laws, we will be punished. We're afraid of God. We say God is loving, but we worry about upsetting God when we disappoint, when we fail, when we don't forgive, when we put ourselves first, when we put ourselves last, when we don't appreciate enough, and when we appreciate too much—too much food, too much wine, too much sex, too much money, too much of anything. What inconsistencies! If we can welcome our own children back into our homes after they've done the despicable, why do we think God won't do the same?

God is never inconsistent. There is no debate. God is consistent in words and deeds. When God says "I love you as you are," quite simply God loves you—as you are. Not only when you're "good," not only w you forgive, not only when you obey… but *always* and *forever!* Unfortunately, many of us create God in our own image rather than accepting that we are created in God's own image.

So what is this "image" of God, and where does it come from?

* * *

Dorothy: As a child, I recall sitting in church on Sundays, gazing at the paintings on the ceiling and the statues placed strategically around the altar. I saw pictures of an old man with a long white beard sitting on a throne with angels kneeling at his feet. I saw an angry man on a boat in a storm with wind whipping through his robes and three or four terrified men hanging onto the sides of the boat, fearing for their very lives. I saw a horrific picture of a man on a cross, with blood dripping from his hands and feet and pouring from his side. I saw lots of clouds and angels with wings. I liked the angels.

I listened as the priest read the Bible. I didn't understand what he read, but I heard his big, booming voice. Then he had a sermon and he yelled at everyone in the church, slamming his fist on the pulpit. He was up really high. I was distracted trying to figure out how he got up on that stand (I couldn't see the stairs from our little pew halfway to the back of the church).

Is it any wonder I promised to be good? I promised to pray every morning and night, and before meals. I promised to go to church on Sundays, and Fridays during Lent. I promised to never talk back to my mother and never tell lies about my sisters. I promised to obey the teacher and always do my homework. I promised to read the Bible, for fifteen minutes a day (that was for bonus points). I promised to never let a boy touch me. I promised to be a nun when I grew up. Maybe I'd live in a cloister. That way I could be really, really good. Does this sound like Fowler's Stage 2 thinking or what?

God did love me—my parents and teachers told me that—but I knew in my heart of hearts that I'd be punished if I wasn't good. I knew that if I died before I had time to confess, I would be punished for a very, very, very long time. I knew that I had to make up for my wrongdoings or there would be trouble!

Some might dismiss my reminiscence as the proverbial "Catholic guilt" syndrome. But Catholics don't have copyright on the fire-and-brimstone wrath of God. If we're honest about our image of God, many have a similar outlook to mine. God's okay, but really, can you trust Him?

Of course you can. I trust God. Jesus is my best friend. When all else in my world is falling apart, I know I can go to God. I have wonderful memories of being part of an active church life throughout my life. All of the important celebrations of my youth and adulthood incorporated religious ritual. These were the most memorable and meaningful experiences of my life, leaving me with an irreplaceable and awe-inspiring sense of the profound and the sacred.

* * *

Hoffman (2005) explained better than many how it is that we're able to hold these inconsistent views of God. He distills the work of many great writers who have attempted to explain how human beings try to understand the unexplainable God. Hoffman suggests our understanding of God is basically twofold. We have a "God concept" and a "God image."

The God concept is based on what we have been taught about God, what we've read, and what people in authority have told us about God (our teachers, our parents, our ministers, our religious leaders, and so on). Our God concept is rational and based on cognitive ideas that we have developed from many sources. People are generally very aware and conscious of their concept of God.

Our God image, on the other hand, is based on what we've experienced about God. It's emotional and experiential. Hoffman suggests that the God image is much more complex than the God concept and may be partially or entirely implicit in nature—that is, we may not even be aware of our God image. It is, however, often what drives and motivates us in our spiritual journey—or lack of, as the case may be. This

God image comes largely from our early relationships with our parents and other significant figures in our lives.

The psychological literature frequently emphasizes the importance of early childhood parental relationships, suggesting that the attachment style we learn in infancy and early childhood affects our adult relationships throughout our lives. There is little doubt that these relationships also affect our image of God.

Attachment theory was first developed by John Bowlby and Mary Ainsworth in the late 60s and 70s. Since then, researchers have applied the theory to many areas of psychological development, including personality, emotional, behavioural, social, and spiritual development. Attachment, used in this sense, isn't the same as emotional bonding. Attachment goes beyond the emotional closeness a mother or father feels toward their infant. Attachment style describes the two-way relationship between an infant and parent that develops over the first two or three years of life.

Attachment theory suggests that infants internalize patterns of interactions with their primary caregivers and these patterns serve as templates for future interpersonal interactions. These templates help the child implicitly understand his or herself in relation to others. This implicit understanding affects behaviour and future development without conscious awareness. The primary caregiver is the first relationship an infant has, and from this relationship the infant learns what to expect in future relationships. The infant develops a way of organizing his or her thoughts, feelings, and behaviours in other close relationships, including God (Noffke & Hall, 2007; Piedmont, 2005).

Infants are completely vulnerable little beings. They come into this big new world entirely dependent on others to meet their basic needs of food, comfort, and care. From a social and biological perspective, the attachment system develops to maintain closeness between the infant and primary caregiver. In order to survive, the infant learns to behave in ways that bring the caregiver closer. In most cases, the primary caregiver is the mother, and her response to the infant's needs results in the infant feeling secure in the world. This sense of security is imperative for the infant to thrive physically, emotionally, and psychologically. It impacts the infant's self-image and personality throughout the lifespan.

There are three main styles of attachment: secure, insecure-resistant (sometimes called anxious-ambivalent), and insecure-avoidant (sometimes called anxious-avoidant).

Infants and young children develop a *secure attachment style* when the mother is caring and loving, consistently providing for the child's physical and emotional needs in a trusting environment. These mothers are highly sensitive to their child's moods and emotions and adjust their parenting behaviour to the child's needs. The infant internalizes the world as a safe place, receiving the message that people are there for them when needed; they are worthy of being cared for and loved. Adults who have developed a secure attachment style in childhood are typically comfortable giving and receiving care, strive for mutual intimacy in adult relationships, and generally describe their relationship with their parents in positive ways.

Infants and young children develop an *insecure-resistant attachment style* when the mother is inconsistent in the care she provides for her child, or perhaps is absent—physically or emotionally—as a result of deficient parenting skills or parental neglect (Simpson, 1999). Perhaps the mother doesn't respond to the infant's cries, responds inconsistently, or is ineffective in soothing the child. Attachment styles develop as a result of the balance between the child's need to feel secure and the need to develop independence and autonomy—that is, to explore the world.

The insecure-resistant infant isn't confident of the mother's availability to provide security in times of distress, and therefore lacks a sense of basic trust and security in the world. Such children may hesitate to leave their mothers' side, or behave inconsistently themselves, approaching the mother for comfort but avoiding her when contact is achieved, expressing obvious ambivalence toward her (Simpson, 1999).

In social psychology, such behaviour is referred to as approach-avoidant behaviour. Something that is desired is also repelled at the same time, thus creating inner conflict (Reber & Reber, 1995). These children come to the conclusion that sometimes their mother is available to meet their needs, and other times not. These children may approach strangers for comfort as readily as their mothers (Weinfield, Sroufe, Egeland & Carlson, 1999) or behave passively when distressed by not actively seeking comfort (Simpson, 1999).

Adults who have developed an insecure-resistant attachment style in childhood lack confidence in the reliable responsiveness of others in adult relationships. They intensely seek intimacy and often express intense anger when others don't respond as desired. They frequently have difficulty making friends and may be prone to heightened feelings of fear, anxiety, and loneliness. They may have a compulsion for self-sacrificing care and yet are dissatisfied with the care others give them (Feeney, 1999). They are much more comfortable giving than receiving, and may even give compulsively. They often describe their fathers as being overly harsh and unfair and believe they have very little control of their own lives.

Infants and young children who grow up in particularly harsh environments develop an *insecure-avoidant attachment style.* Their parents or caregivers are detached, consistently unresponsive, distressed, or hostile. Children who develop avoidant attachment may have consistently cold and rejecting parents who either have an aversion to close bodily contact or, conversely, overstimulate their infants. These children may have suffered some form of physical or emotional abuse (Simpson, 1999). In such an environment, the infant internalizes the world as a frightening place, a place where people cannot be trusted, receiving the message that they are not worth loving.

Adults who have an insecure-avoidant attachment style typically fear intimacy and have a tendency to maintain emotional distance in "close" relationships and rarely open up to share their deep personal feelings with another person. Because of their low trust, they have difficulty fostering meaningful relationships. They are unable to give or receive care and have a particularly pessimistic view of relationships. They may not even believe that true love exists (Feeney, 1999). In fact, neurobiological research suggests that because their parents weren't in tune with their emotional needs as young children, over time this emotional neglect caused the children to develop an implicit (nonconscious) mental representation of relationships that makes emotional closeness particularly uncomfortable (Nofke & Hall, 2007). Adults with avoidant attachment often have difficulty recalling specific experiences from their childhood, which may result in an idealized version of their relationship with their parents.

A number of psychologists have applied the attachment style model of relationships to understanding how one's image of God develops. As you might expect, those with secure attachment see God as comforting and secure and those with avoidant styles of attachment often avoid an emotional relationship with God. Because of the uncomfortable and stressful experience of emotional attachment, avoidant adults have a tendency to intellectualize their relationship with God, hence keeping God at a distance and remaining self-sufficient, which is what they learned as children. Their God concept is separate and dissociated from their God image (Nofke & Hall, 2007).

Surprisingly, those with resistant attachment styles, over time, are often inclined to search for security and stability in a relationship with God. In this sense, their relationship with God seems to compensate for what's lacking in their human relationships. They seek closeness with God rather than their typical detached and ambivalent human relationships (Kirkpatrick, 1998). No doubt there are multiple factors that influence whether a person seeks a relationship with God and what this might look like. However, at the beginning of one's spiritual journey, these typically consistent attachment patterns are likely to operate automatically, as they do in other close personal relationships.

You can see from the complex nature of human development, and the distinction between the God concept and God image, that it is very easy to have an inconsistent notion of what God is like. You may have been told that God is kind and loving, but if you've experienced only harsh and non-loving relationships, these notions will transfer to your ideas about God. The God concept and God image develop in parallel (Hoffman, 2005), although for many the God image remains at an implicit, unconscious level in the psyche.

We hold both an external and internal image of God, simultaneously (Nofke & Hall, 2007). Our external image is comparable to the God concept, which is rational, and we are consciously aware of this image. Our internal image is comparable to the God image and is relational, which may be implicit—that is, we may not be aware of it. What we're taught and know about God will influence our experiences of God, and vice versa.

What makes the entire process even more complicated is that we aren't taught just one notion of God; there are many, and sometimes conflicting, ideas about God. Similarly, we don't experience just one type of relationship; we have many significant relationships in our lives. Most would argue that it's impossible for any human to love consistently and unconditionally. Moreover, the unconscious (implicit) knowledge we gain about God comes from many sources: relationships, feelings, art, music, and culture.

Yes, what we're told about God influences our experiences. But Hoffman (2005) clearly demonstrates the limitations of our God concept when he says that one can change one's thoughts about a situation, but this doesn't change how he or she experiences the situation. Similarly, one can change one's thoughts about God, but this doesn't necessarily change one's experience of God. "If cognitions do not contain some *experience,* they will be unable to touch the *God Image*" (Hoffman, 2005, p. 134).

Intellectual knowledge of God isn't sufficient. In fact, intellectual knowledge absent of experience can create a faith crisis. Furthermore, discrepancies between our God concept and God image can lead to spiritual neurosis founded on guilt and shame (Hoffman, 2005). The individual will most often internalize blame if he or she is taught that God is loving but experiences God as distant. The dissociation, or fracture, between the rational God concept and the relational God image can only be reconciled if the God image is brought into conscious awareness, and this can only happen through experience.

From a psychological perspective, we need to create new neural networks that are formed by experiencing others as responsive and caring and ourselves as loved (Nofke & Hall, 2007). From a spiritual perspective, we need to foster direct, emotionally laden experiences with God that transform our implicit representations of God, which are a result of maladaptive human attachment figures (Noffke & Hall, 2007).

There are no perfect human relationships. All of our human relationships are maladaptive at some level.

Nonetheless, these relationships are the foundation of our images of God, whether they're explicit or implicit—that is, conscious or unconscious—notions of what or who God may be. The only way we can align our God concept and God image is through experience.

THE *Invitation*

chapter six

A man dies and goes to heaven. Of course, St. Peter meets him at the pearly gates.

"Here's how it works," St. Peter says. "You need one hundred points to make it into heaven. Tell me all the good things you've done and I'll give you a certain number of points for each item, depending on how good it was. When you reach a hundred points, you get in."

"Okay," the man says. "I was married to the same woman for fifty years and never cheated on her, even in my heart."

"That's wonderful," says St. Peter. "That's worth three points!"

"Three points?" he says. "Well, I attended church all my life and supported its ministry with my tithe and service."

"Terrific!" says St. Peter. "That's certainly worth a point."

"One point? Golly. How about this: I started a soup kitchen in my city and worked in a shelter for homeless veterans."

"Fantastic, that's good for two more points."

"Two points!" the man cries. "At this rate, the only way I'll get into heaven is by the grace of God!"

St. Peter smiles. "Come on in."

> *For there is no distinction, since all have sinned and fall short of the glory of God; they are now justified by his grace as a gift, through the redemption that is in Christ Jesus.* (Romans 3:23–24, NRSV)

Frank: Where do we find this grace of God? What does it look like? What does it mean to experience God? Where do we look for answers? What is right? What's the point, anyway? Does it make any difference in my life, or is it all just feel-good talk and intellectualizing?

I've heard it said that a person can [illegible] spiritual relationship with God in three ways [illegible] seat, on your feet, and on your knees. On your seat implies studying and reading spiritual books. On your feet implies doing good deeds. On your knees implies praying and meditating on the presence of God in your life.

I invite those who are looking for something real, for that emotionally laden experience of God, to journey with Scripture. Scripture is called the soul of theology, the soul of faith-seeking understanding, the soul of how to know Jesus and God. In the Scriptures, you will undoubtedly find your God and the freedoms and peace Jesus so often talked about.

* * *

There are two main ways to read Scripture—one through study, the other through prayer. One of the arguments we've often heard about reading Scripture is that it, too, is inconsistent. We've heard many people use the First Testament (often referred to as the Old Testament) to support their own prejudices. There are many statements in the First Testament that support wars, bodily mutilation, and horrific degradation of women. For example, in the book of Sirach 42:14, the prophet says, *"Better is the wickedness of a man than a woman who does good; it is woman who brings shame and disgrace"* (NRSV). That's pretty awful language, if taken literally.

Jesus came to fulfill the promises of the First Testament. For every prophecy in the First Testament, Jesus responds in the Second Testament (often referred to as the New Testament). In John 8:3–10, we have another story about a woman caught in adultery. Verse ten finishes with Jesus' response:

> *Jesus straightened up and said to her, "Woman, where are they? Has no one condemned you?"*
> *She said, "No one, sir."*
> *And Jesus said, "Neither do I condemn you. Go your way…"* (John 8:10–1, NRSV)

Now, Jesus' view of women presents quite a different picture.

Merely *reading* Scripture can add to our inconsistent view of who God is and can sometimes confuse us with contradictory messages. When approaching Scripture, we need to seek the truth with an open and Spirit-filled stance of love based on credible study and reflection.

We most often rely on scholars to interpret the Holy Bible for us. The expert always has the edge. But the Bible is also referred to as the "Living Word." If the Bible is alive, then it must speak to everyone in a vibrant and relevant form. Although truth is found in the revelations of the Scriptures, our human limitations preclude us from recognizing this truth at times. Because of our human limitations, the Bible, the

Living Word, is thus a dynamic process of revelation and development based on our understanding of who God is for God's people. It takes time and is a personal journey.

God is relational and the Divine project for each one of us is uncovered in Jesus. And it is only through Scripture that we can find out who Jesus is. As Christians, we can only understand the First Testament in the context of the Second Testament. The Second Testament fulfills and completes the First Testament.

Jesus shows us who God is. Jesus' words and actions were *always* totally consistent and therefore point us in a confident direction toward God, a direction of harmony, joy, and peace. God doesn't want you to be perfect. God does want you to be a good person. God has no agenda, hidden or otherwise. God wants only to love you and for you to experience the fullness of that love.

Father/Mother God images in Scripture point to a parent's love for his or her child. When Jesus prayed, he called out "Abba"—meaning "Daddy" in Aramaic, the language he spoke. Abba was a term used by children, by toddlers who trusted their father. The Abba/Imma (Father/Mother) image of God calls you to grow in your own understanding of a loving relationship with your God, and to even surpass and develop new initiatives toward your God. The parent doesn't want the child to stay a child forever.

The parent delights in the child asking questions, in trying new things, in growing and developing. The parent-to-child example of a loving relationship is the closest thing we as human beings can experience to understand the tremendous love God has for us all.

Remember that it's okay to question God. God isn't threatened by your questions, your meanderings. God delights in your inquisitiveness. If you neither lack faith nor have doubts, how can you understand? If you have desires and questions, this shows you have an active Spirit and God is calling you forward to respond. If you're dissatisfied with the answers people give you, conduct your own search. It's good to search out answers to your questions, but it's wise to rely on past scholarship and expertise as a guide. The quest for a deeper life experience points us in new directions of wisdom and personal fulfillment. To understand your own spiritual journey, though, is to go beyond the satisfaction of intellectualization. It must be integrated with your life experiences and written in your heart.

> *Within them I shall plant my Law, writing it on their hearts. Then I shall be their God and they will be my people.* (Jeremiah 31:33, NJB)

Remember, the longest journey in a person's search is from the head to the heart. It's not a task to be taken lightly. It's a lifelong quest.

What are we looking for? Do we not all yearn for acceptance, support, affirmation, approval, and a sense of worth, nurturing, and love? These are the very things that a healthy relationship with Jesus brings. Yes, some religious experiences can conjure feelings of closeness to God. God's Spirit is always alive and well, sometimes responding in powerful ways. The feelings of elation soon begin to wither and eventually die out. They feed us less and less as time goes on.

Paradoxically, the more we look for feelings in our prayers, the less they seem to be there. Perhaps this is God's way of calling us to a deeper relationship. Hanging one's hat, so to speak, on these highs is like hoping the honeymoon lasts forever in a marriage. Unless we transcend the emotional experiences and grow, moving our connection with our image of God from an imminent surface relationship to a deep transcendent personal relationship, we soon lose desire and life again becomes mundane. Remember, in an active love relationship, a person either draws closer to the other or pulls further away. Relationships are seldom dormant. We need to spend time nurturing a friendship. In order to know someone, we must spend time together.

We may once in a while feel a sense of God's presence through nature, as in experiencing the beauty of a fantastic sunset or witnessing the magnificence of a snow-topped mountain, but to carry a heartfelt union, a companionship, we need to know God ime and maturity. If we are to be complete, we must first admit that we need a spiritual component in our lives. Jesus is always knocking. We only have to say yes for the door to be opened! If you want a friend, you have to be a friend. We need time and commitment to have opportunities to get to know someone. This personal experience is complemented at times by our institutional church experience. But we must look deeper than a Sunday morning model of church in order to develop a personal experience of God. We must enter into a continuous, ongoing relationship, and whether felt or not, we know the relationship is there and we can depend on it. It's a choice that we make, and once made, God will never let us down.

We draw life not from what's happening externally, where we could become egotistical and nurture our false self-conscience, but from a calm light that lives inside. This calm light inside us continually becomes stronger and more recognizable to us personally, although externally it is only recognizable periodically. At times, God's companionship and action in our lives is seen more clearly than at other times.

> *Again Jesus spoke to them, saying, "I am the light of the world. Whoever follows me will never walk in darkness but will have the light of life."* (John 8:12, NRSV)

I have come as light into the world, so that everyone who believes in me should not remain in the darkness. (John 12:46, NRSV)

Jesus said to him, "I am the way, and the truth, and the life. No one comes to the Father except through me. If you know me, you will know my Father also." (John 14:6–7, NRSV)

...and after the fire a sound of sheer silence. When Elijah heard it, he wrapped his face in his mantle and went out... (1 Kings 19:12–13, NRSV)

Sit in silence, and go into darkness. (Isaiah 47:5, NRSV)

It is good for one to bear the yoke in youth, to sit alone in silence when the Lord has imposed it. (Lamentations 3:27–28, NRSV)

Very early the next morning, long before daylight, Jesus got up and left the house. He went out of town to a lonely place, where He prayed. (Mark 1:35, TEV)

At that time Jesus went up a hill to pray and spent the whole night there praying to God. (Luke 6:12, TEV)

This transcendent experience of God's friendship is a truth that leaves our inner selves with an experience of confidence, of knowing what's real, and of full acceptance. It's like a touch of gentleness after an awe experience of nature, or an intimate sacred encounter with another human being. Such is this mystical relationship with your God.

So why is such a friendship so rare? If God's always knocking and we're spiritual beings, craving this meaningful relationship, why do so few experience it? What creates the block in our humanity? Surely God didn't create a complicated maze of discernment processes through which only a few can manoeuvre. This book is about spirituality for the ordinary person. It's about a journey, a journey toward freedom—psychological and spiritual freedom.

The idea of freedom is enticing. Advertisers are constantly offering promises of freedom—freedom from financial worries, freedom from relationship woes, freedom from wrinkles, freedom from illness, and so on. But when it comes to the journey of life, we all know there are no instant solutions, no instant gratifications, no utopia. Even if we live the intent of prayer and develop a close relationship with God, as St Paul says:

> *...even considering the exceptional character of the revelations [Paul experienced]. Therefore, to keep me [Paul] from being too elated, a thorn was given me in the flesh, a messenger... Three*

> *times I appealed to the Lord about this,*
> *would leave me, but he said to me, "My*
> *is sufficient for you, for power is made perfect in weakness."* (2 Corinthians 12:7–9, NRSV)

St. Paul was humbled to surrender to his human weakness and could only move toward peace through acceptance, surrender, and trust in God. Unless we can transcend ourselves—that is, our compulsions toward self-indulgence, excess, power, and control—and be able to surrender to God's love in total trust, we won't experience the true freedom and peace our gracious God offers us.

The idea is that rather than responding to life out of our own brokenness and self-centred motivations, we gently face life with positive thoughts, dreams, and aspirations and make our movements in life be motivated by love, compassion, and self-affection. Yes, self-affection, for by caring for ourselves we energize our hearts and souls to engage with life and others, as God purposed us to do. Unconditional love is the greatest source of energy, a lot more than can ever be realized by any selfish energy. God's unconditional love is very demanding. God's yes is absolute, total, unlike our yes, which is problematic—we have yeses and nos both at the same time:

> *Was I vacillating when I wanted to do this? Do I make my plans according to ordinary human*

> *standards, ready to say, "Yes, yes" and "No, no" at the same time? As surely as God is faithful our word to you has not been "Yes and No." For the Son of God, Jesus Christ, whom we proclaimed among you… but in him it is always "Yes." For in him every one of God's promises is a "Yes."* (2 Corinthians 1:17–20, NRSV)

Our premise with this book is to show that our personal life mission is first and foremost to be in a relationship with our God—in other words, to be mystics, to be saints! Our remaining values and necessities of life will then fall into place naturally.

> *Set your hearts on his kingdom first, and on God's saving justice, and all these other things will be given you as well.* (Matthew 6:33, NJB)

Easier said than done! A few short decades ago, a family could live quite comfortably with one income. The husband, generally the main breadwinner, could financially support his wife at home, four or five children, a car payment, a house payment, and perhaps a family vacation every year or so. Are we sure this age of technology, disposable everything, and quick-fix remedies are affording us a better way of life? We now see young couples both working furiously with two car payments, a house payment, drowning in debt, and still having no room for children in the equation.

Perhaps households will soon contain more than the nuclear family. This frenzy of life fuels excessive psychological stress and constant noise, causing us to slowly disintegrate and move further and further away from our centre. And yet it is at our centre that we find our relationship with God.

No wonder we have restless spirits. We are fragmented. We are all experiencing multiple personalities. At work we are driven to succeed, to strive for more money, to earn that big promotion, to buy more toys. At home we put on a façade that we actually care. We try to keep the things alive that we think are still important to us—a nice family, a good-looking wife, a well-dressed husband, a beautiful home, family vacations, and children who excel in school, in sports, and in the arts.

This is quite a tall order. When we're alone, we allow our weaknesses to surface, our pacifiers—whatever we crave—to control us again. We think to ourselves, *I deserve this once in a while, damn it!* Our dreams and fantasies take us to more questionable desires at times: *Why can't I have what I want? I deserve it.*

In spite of all we have said, it's all about the money!

Where or when does it all become still, silent, and calm? The battle of the sexes continues with our encounters with women and men. The battle of finances takes away all our energy as we work many, many hours to sustain a living. The battle of our own agmentation drives us in directions we'd rather not go. We're mentally overloaded and psychologically deficient. It seems impossible for our minds to rest and be calm. Our very beings live in constant restlessness, driven by mental anxiety. But God knows our troubles, our pain, our weaknesses, our worries:

> *Surely life is more than food, and the body more than clothing! Look at the birds in the sky. They do not sow or reap or gather into barns; yet your heavenly Father feeds them. Are you not worth much more than they are? …So do not worry about tomorrow: tomorrow will take care of itself. Each day has enough trouble of its own.* (Matthew: 6:25–26, 34, NJB)

We must acquire the conditions of God—be Godlike in our words and actions, having the mind of Jesus—without losing our own identity. This will help us to become even more truly who we are meant to be. Saint Teresa of Avila, a famous mystic from Spain, once wrote that if we search to know ourselves we end up in the arms of Jesus. Truly knowing and loving yourself leads you to Jesus.

Many people get caught up in a vice or addiction—such as alcohol, drugs, power, sex, eating, or gambling—in a desperate pursuit to achieve freedom. The pleasures of humanity create the pains of tomorrow. One decision in life can affect us for our whole lives. Unfortunately, the addiction bec an entrapment that destroys freedom. But there is freedom. There is real spiritual and psychological freedom.

One of the worst things to fight in our psyche is the power of your mistress, those addictions that consume your thoughts, energy, and emotions until you get your next fix. Your compulsions to buy or eat; sexuality; addictions to drugs, alcohol, and gambling; and compulsive perceptions of greed, power, selfishness, and fear are all powers outside your centre. They all drive you crazy!

Go ahead. Be involved in an obsessive behaviour that fragments your being. It works for a while. That's why we do it. But if you do, you'll soon discover the *limitations of life*. You'll soon learn that *sin corrects itself*, and hopefully at some point you'll want to come back and rediscover yourself, who you really are and who you're meant to become. Then, once you know yourself again, you'll have second thoughts about doing something solely for the sake of some lost moment of pleasure. Freedom is when you control your compulsions, not when they control you.

Obsessions and addictions drive the psyche to chaos, securing that you're always connected to something other than a place of peace. We're all starving from having no time, no quiet, or no love. Does anybody really care about us? Who ever really stops to listen to our hearts? Is nurturing and caring for each other through time and compassion a thing of the past? Have we really succumbed to the noise and busyness of our abusive existence?

This Scripture passage provides an insight into what can happen to our spirit, and inadvertently to our whole being, if we aren't concerned with what we allow into our person:

> *When the unclean spirit has gone out of a person, it wanders through waterless regions looking for a resting place, but not finding any, it says, "I will return to my house from which I came." When it comes, it finds it swept and put in order. Then it goes and brings seven other spirits more evil than itself, and they enter and live there; and the last state of that person is worse than the first.* (Luke 11:24–26, NRSV)

We are made in God's image with intellect and free will to choose our destiny. We can destroy ourselves with worldly excesses and so-called finite pleasures, living a shallow surface life, or we can taste God's peace and joy through a life with interior depth and harmony.

> *For where your treasure is, there your heart will be also.* (Matthew 6:21, NRSV)

We are all invited to access the only source of life experience that can be relied on, the only source that's always totally trustworthy and totally cor mystical, deeply spiritual, comfortably relationship with our gracious God. In c to transcend the chaos that takes us away from our own essence and wholeness, we need God.

> *Jesus answered them, "Have faith [trust] in God."* (Mark 11:22, NRSV)

Trust God. Believe in God. That's the leap we have to make. God is safe. Look to Jesus to show you who God is. Jesus' life was about more than money, more than relationships and psychological overload. It was about being insightful, having an awareness of the calm and beauty in front of him, about caring, loving, and listening to all of life and the disharmony it contained and responding to it with love and gentleness. For each moment of our existence, let us think about, as a friend once wrote to me, "being the people God wants us to be. Weaknesses pull us in many directions. We must be focused on one direction in our hearts and minds" (Evelyn Glover, personal communication).

A person's truth speaks to who that person is in relationship with—the world, nature, or other people. People clarify who they are through direct personal experiences and relationships. By developing an informed conscience, we become attuned to our own personal truth. Only then can an individual's truth stand alone. It is then to be observed and critiqued from all angles. A person's truth, one's conscience, is the guide. Our conscience must be informed by credible external sources and in relationship with the Holy Spirit within each of us. We don't just change our lives for another set of rules. Consequently, truth of conscience and Spirit remains constant from one generation to the next.

The way truth is interpreted by individuals can sometimes be problematic and life-stifling rather than life-giving. In our fast-paced world, with new discoveries occurring almost every minute of the day, how can we say anything survives from one generation to the next? Spirituality—defined as our own personal relationship with God—is such a constant, a major aspect of who we are as human persons. It is personal and relational. All spirituality is a response to God's initiative. It can never be wrong. It is one's own personal relationship with one's own personal God. Who can judge how that relationship should look other than the individual?

We've been talking about a journey. We use the word *journey* to describe life because life is a process, or movement, toward a goal. Most people follow the social norms, so their journeys unfold somewhat automatically, so to speak, without conscious awareness of the decisions that affect their lives. Carl Jung, a Swiss psychiatrist and one of the founders of analytical psychology, believed society in general would benefit if individuals achieved a stronger appreciation of their own inner promptings and thus be “less susc to mass ideologies” (Bianchi, 1988, p. 21)– that is, societal norms. But only when we embark on an inward journey do we have the strength to step outside of these social norms.

At times, especially during a crisis or major life event (such as a death, illness, financial troubles, or birth of a child), we reassess our direction in life and make it more meaningful. We can choose to run on autopilot and not pursue this inward journey. This is, of course, up to the individual. However, if you’re looking for something more meaningful than the status quo, or something that provides life and joy beyond working ten or fourteen hours a day to simply meet your basic needs, this journey is well worth pursuing. Your life will progress, regardless of your choices. It can simply be an instinctual process of maturity and aging—a fast-paced, quite ordinary, and possibly pleasant experience—or it can far exceed the ordinary, if you choose. It can be a deep experience of love and awareness, full of insights, peace, and joy.

> Now, that which enables one to live together with another person is chiefly friendship. As the Philosopher [Aristotle] says in the *Ethics*: “each person spending his time with his friend, doing the things they like best, wishing to live together as a friend with the one who has a high regard for his kind of life.” Thus, some people

go hunting together, others drink together, still others devote themselves to philosophy, and so on.... It was consequently necessary that some sort of friendship with God be made available, so that we might live together with Him..." (Thomas Aquinas, as cited in Bourke, 1964, p. 364)

THE Response

chapter seven

Frank: When I was training for ministry, a pastor I worked with told me the story of a man who was grieving terribly due to family loss. The man was a farmer, a good man who worked hard, enjoyed a beer after a hard day's work, and was always ready to lend a helping hand to the neighbours if they needed it. One summer, right in the middle of harvest, his four-year-old son was killed in a farm accident when the neighbour backed his truck out of the quonset and didn't see the boy playing in a puddle just behind the truck.

The pastor went to see this man and his wife to offer condolences, and also to see if there was anything he could do to give them hope and comfort. The farmer felt awkward because he wasn't a regular at Sunday services but nonetheless he greeted the pastor pleasantly and shared his grief and feelings of helplessness.

A few years later, the pastor made a second visit to the same man, following an even greater tragedy. His wife and youngest son were killed by a drunk driver. The pastor knocked on the door one evening about a week after the funeral and the farmer opened the door slowly. Clearly he had been drinking and he looked a lot thinner than he had a few years earlier. The farmer invited the pastor into the house and they both sat down at the kitchen table. The oldest son offered coffee, then left to go to his room.

The pastor tried to offer some words of comfort, but the man just looked at him with emptiness and sorrow in his eyes.

"Why? Why would God do this to me?" he asked. "I have no strength or will left to live. I don't know what I'd do without Luke, my oldest boy."

The pastor prayed with him and left the house with a heavy heart, knowing he didn't have the words or answers to make the man feel better. He prayed for the man after that, hoping that God would give him inner peace, acceptance, and the strength to move on with his life.

They lived in a small community and word travelled quickly that the oldest son was becoming quite a character around town. Suffice it to say that his name was well-known among the local law enforcement. About four years later, Luke's reckless behaviour took its toll. He ran a train signal and was killed instantly when the train couldn't stop in time.

Once more, the pastor set out to visit the farmer, praying all the while that the Spirit would somehow inspire him when he got to the farm. When he arrived, the farmer was out in the yard, working on his combine, getting ready for the late summer's harvest. When the pastor approached, the once gentle farmer turned on him, yelled, and swore that he should get off his property and never come back. He'd had it with the pastor's pious visits and so-called prayers that did no good and only seemed to accentuate the pain and suffering in the farmer's life. He'd had it with this so-called "god" and promises of peace and comfort. There was no God as far as he was concerned and, if there was, he wasn't interested in a God who would take three sons and his wife.

"Don't come back!" the farmer shouted. "And if you do, you'll wish you hadn't."

Why did the pastor tell me this story? I think he was trying to tell me that sometimes there are no answers for people. Sometimes bad stuff, horrible stuff, happens and sometimes it feels more like a kick in the groin than an invitation from God. In the last chapter, we talked about the invitation to enter into a deeper relationship with God, who promises a more meaningful life as opposed to working hard to support our material existence. I don't buy it! If it were that easy, more people would do it. If we just have to say yes, then why aren't people saying yes? Why aren't more people responding to the invitation? We suggested that because of the fast-paced, high-stress world we live in, people just don't have the time and energy to nurture friendship with God. There's more to it than that.

There are many reasons people aren't living this mystical life we've been talking about. Some are angry with God, and rightfully so. The farmer in this story has every right to be angry with God. He experienced more tragedy and pain in his life than I ever have—more than I can imagine, in fact. Some have had a bad experience with church. Look at the number of lawsuits we hear about in the media because of sexual abuse by clergy. Some have suffered painful childhoods with parents who were so strict about religion that their children wouldn't step one foot into a church, much less pray at home. Some people don't believe in the payout. They have no role models demonstrating this inner peace and joy. The light just isn't shining! Some simply have no desire. They're content, happy with their life, happy with the status quo. What's the matter with ordinary? Isn't God in the ordinary, too? Some just don't know how. There are as many reasons as there are people. We each have our own way of manoeuvring through life's challenges. We develop coping skills and we're experts at rationalizing our choices.

Whatever the reasons, be assured—it's *okay!* God loves you as you are, where you are, and how you are! How do *we* know this? How can *you* know this? Just look at the Scriptures; look at Jesus' words and deeds. Nowhere in Scripture does Jesus condemn or turn his back. Jesus shows us how much God loves us. But don't believe us—find out for yourself.

What if you aren't the scripture-reading kinda guy? (That's *okay*, by the way.) Something in your heart has drawn you to this book. What is that something? Psychologists, sociologists, and anthropologists agree that the human person is biological, psychological, sociological, and spiritual. We're compelled to nourish each of these aspects in our daily lives. The first three—biological, psychological, and sociological needs—are more obvious than spiritual needs. More concrete. I don't think anyone would disagree that we need to nourish our bodies with healthy lifestyle choices; that we need human touch, love, and affection to nourish our psyches; and that we need friendship, community, and belonging to be nourished sociologically. What do spiritual needs look like? How do people nourish their spiritual needs? How do people find meaning in their lives?

I ask my university students these questions and always find it interesting to hear their responses. I ask whether meaning and spirituality are the same, whether we can have one without the other. Inevitably, these young adults have as many answers as there are students in the class. I've come to the conclusion that meaning is a very personal experience. It seems the consensus is that one can find meaning without conscious spiritual awareness, but rarely, if ever, does one find spiritual awareness without meaning.

* * *

Bookshelves in libraries or bookstores are full of authors who have written on subjects such as how to live a meaningful life, how to deal with pain (physical, emotional, and psychological), and how to change. The psychological research on the topic of what contributes to a meaningful life is diverse as well.

Personality psychologist Robert Emmons spent the better part of his career researching well-being, happiness, meaning, human potential, and personal goals. After decades of research, he concluded that he couldn't ignore spirituality. In fact, he made the bold statement that to ignore spirituality in understanding human nature and personality would be the equivalent of "academic malpractice" (Emmon, 1999, p. 7). He said that, for many people, spirituality is what makes their life "meaningful, valuable, and purposeful" (Emmon, 1999, p. 7).

People express their need and desire for a meaningful existence in different ways. Some say they're looking for happiness, others for satisfaction, hope, and quality of life. However, the experts who study these constructs have found empirical evidence that spirituality is unique and cannot be ignored in attempting to understand the human person (Emmons, 1999; Pargament, Magyar-Russell & Murray-Swank, 2005).

To say that spirituality is unique means that spirituality is not the same as happiness, not the same as hope, not the same as any measure of life satisfaction. According to psychology, spirituality contributes something unique to personal and social functioning. What makes it unique is that we're dealing with the sacred, something beyond the realm of secular measures, and, according to many theorists, "it is not merely one part of living. It is the core of life" (Pargament et al., 2005, p. 668). These authors quote the great historian and philosopher Eliade (1957):

> The sacred is equivalent to a power and, in the last analysis, to reality. The sacred is saturated with being. Sacred power means reality and at the same time enduringness and

> efficacity.... The religious individual, Eliade goes on to note, desires to participate in that reality, remaining as long as possible in a sacred universe. (Pargament et al., 2005, pp. 668–669)

The meaningfulness one experiences in living the sacred is more enduring and efficacious than any other motivation or human goal. Emmons (and others) found that striving for the spiritual is more strongly correlated with human well-being than any other measure of personal strivings included in their research, including intimacy and close personal relationships. Emmons speaks of the necessity to include spirituality measures in psychological research that aim to understand the human person, but interestingly he also states that he himself does not have any professional interest in religious beliefs.

Even from an objective, empirical perspective, we cannot ignore our spiritual being.

> Spirituality must be seen as the all embracing, all encompassing, totally inclusive part of the human, out of which all else physical, mental, and emotional flows... It is in this context that we begin to understand many of the great theologians and many of the great philosophers who spoke of the human being as a unified whole. (Cox, 2005, p. 38)

So why say yes to God's invitation? Beca saying yes is to deny (or ignore) the very core o being. You are made in God's own image. And God's own image is one of love. The invitation is to get to know yourself in light of God's own loving nature, which ultimately will lead you to knowing God. James Allen, an early twentieth-century author, wrote:

> We become spiritually rich, when we discover the adventure within; when we are conscious of the oneness of all life; when we know the power of meditation; when we experience kinship with nature. (Allen, edited 1968, p. 11)

First and foremost, we have to see the value and importance of self-affection. We must be gentle with ourselves, accepting the importance of our biological, psychological, social, and spiritual needs. The invitation is to experience life with a sensitive appreciation for beauty in nature, art, and architecture. This is our call—not individualism, materialism, power, or self-serving fantasies of life, but real dreams and experiences of God's freedoms and the gifts created for our pleasure, to appreciate a taste of life at its finest. Paul Tillich, a great theologian who dealt with the psychological aspects of human existence, wrote that "God" is where we find human wholeness rather than fragmentation (Cox, 2005).

We need to find value once more in the human person, in simply being, in simply enjoying being. We need to consciously rebuke the temptation to get absorbed into meaningless strivings. Essentially, we have moved from an industrial society that valued material possessions to a technological society that values knowledge. We value the speed of accessing information, of evaluating existing products, and of creating new platforms. We can send and receive information around the world instantaneously. In our technological age, saying yes to a relationship with God, to the mystical journey, is to put the brakes on busyness and psychic noise. We need to slow down and move inward; we need time to contemplate and just *be.* We need to love ourselves and accept that God loves us.

This journey inward can be a frightful notion. We're all broken and we've all been affected by pain, some more than others. When our hearts are full of pain from loss of love, relationship, or our jobs, when what is truly important to us is taken away, we can become so lonely that we're obsessed with despair, aloneness, and misunderstandings, soon becoming trapped in a valley of desolation, depression, and emptiness. In these worst-case scenarios, we're often unable to escape the pain on our own. We need other people to reach down into that abysmal hole of darkness and love us with more love than the level of brokenness and pain we are experiencing; only then are we able to proceed onward on a journey of healing toward life. We need a community—people around us who care enough to journey with us. As God's people, created in God's image and likeness, we're meant to spend the majority of our experiences in community and in peace, being free.

To be *free* is to be able to make choices for ourselves. God has given us intellect and free will. We are free to decide which road to take, which path to follow. We are free to decide whether we want to remain trapped in a life of shallow busyness or experience a life of meaningfulness and depth. We are free to choose to enjoy a life of peace, harmony, and fulfillment. The movement toward freedom begins in the interior, then moves to the exterior reality of our life. Freedom isn't found in exterior worldly obsessions or pleasures. If we only hang out on the outside of life (the external pleasures), we'll only experience a self-serving and essentially self-starving surface existence. Wayne Dyer, a well-known contemporary author, quotes Herman Melville's *Moby Dick*, calling this the "half-lived life":

> The half-lived life is lived exclusively in the trappings and the structures that are the outer world. These are the horrors that Melville tells us encompass the soul, as if one were unable to find the center where bliss resides. You sense that there is a deeper, richer experience of life available, yet you somehow continue

> to flail around in the external ocean, glimpsing that verdant Tahiti, that peaceful chapel from a distance.
>
> Perhaps the most devastating scenario imaginable is to face death knowing that because of some imagined fear, you have always chosen a half-lived life in which you avoided doing the things your heart beckoned you to do. I urge you to change the scenario now. Start living your life with the courage to step ashore and experience your insular Tahiti. (Dyer, 1998, p. 146)

This interior place, motivated by our heart and soul in relationship with God, brings us real life. Our spiritual life brings us freedom.

Remember Jesus' words:

> *Therefore I tell you, do not worry about your life, what you will eat or what you will drink, or about your body, what you will wear. Is not life more than food, and the body more than clothing?* (Matthew 6:25, NRSV)

WHERE TO *Start*

chapter eight

Dear Frank:

Well, for what it's worth, I impart to you my observations at this point in life. Now, of course, it's only my observations based on my journey to date.

Being in your forties is like being halfway across a river. It doesn't make a hell of a lot of difference whether you swim to one shore or another.

Your forties will see your ambition and reality collide.

Your forties will see you reexamine your past, your present, and your future. That's not surprising, considering that life is a timed event…

Joyful events are fleeting; unfortunately, pain tends to hang around as long as you want it to.

Being humble in life and having a sense of humility puts a healthier perspective on life.

When your employer gives you a paycheque at the end of the month, he is paying you for your time. The question is not whether he got full value but whether you got full value. You have basically given him a chunk of your life…

It may feel good to give, but don't forget to take a little bit along the way.

When somebody says that they're introducing more technology in your life, that usually means you'll be running faster…

Don't speed through small towns.

Buy and listen to a lot of Van Morrison CDs.

Don't bring a knife to a gunfight and hope to survive.

If you're
need I say r
You'll r
appreciate
thing.
For al
end of t
to all. F
word "f
Tall
Remember to look
—Ray

So where do you start on your inward journey? Does your search start in your forties, as Ray implies in his reflection, or in your fifties, or your thirties, or your twenties? The premise is that you have a desire to look for more. The desire may come in little twinges of wondering why, in waves of overwhelming responsibility, or perhaps in the pains of dissatisfaction with the choices you've made or the hand you've been dealt. The minute you settle for less than you deserve, you get even less than you settled for. You can choose to look for more. Age is of no consequence.

The beginning of the journey is the choice to believe there's more than the mundane. The journey, then, will take you through three levels of truth: the truth of self, the truth of others, and the truth of God (Maddux, 1977, cited in Robb, 1983). The truth of

rselves at an emotionally hon-
goes beyond "the false sense of
(Thomas Merton, as cited in Robb,
oneself requires self-reflection, quiet,
ness to accept the naked truth about what
t requires listening to others, a skill which
s beyond our own survival instincts and de-
veness. When we're threatened, the fight-or-flight
rvival instinct clicks in automatically, so expect re-
sistance. True self-knowledge inevitably threatens us, but ultimately takes us to a place of humility, of seeing our weaknesses in humility and celebrating our giftedness, again in humility.

A young woman told me a story about an experience she had on a trip to a tropical resort. Early one evening, she was walking along the beach—alone. She sat on a rock and watched the never-ending waves roll onto the shore, lapping against the rock she sat on. It was mesmerizing.

Time passed quickly and before she knew it the sunset was long gone. She found her mind drifting—and then came the tears. She knew not where they came from, except that it was from such a deep place within that she felt separate from them. She felt herself letting go and, as she let go, she could see the waves removing something from her core and taking it out to sea, something that seemed like green slime. She felt lighter and lighter; the tears seemed to cleanse her of this horrible substance.

Eventually, she had no more tears in her; the warm night breeze gave her renewed life and renewed breath. She left that experience knowing that something profound had happened to her that evening. She had no cognizant understanding of what had occurred, but on some profound level she now knew the truth of her own goodness and beauty.

The journey of self-awareness isn't always this profound and it never ends. It requires continuous reflection and openness to others. The truth of our self ultimately leads us to the truth of others. Seeing ourselves in honesty and humility helps us to see others in a stance of acceptance and compassion. When we're less judgmental of our own weaknesses and foibles, we're able to be less judgmental of others. We come to realize that we're much like the people we criticize, leading us to become more tolerant of others. Compassion, then, becomes our companion. The truth of others is that human nature is less than perfect and yet more beautiful than we could ever imagine.

The truth of self and the truth of others necessarily leads us to the truth of God. Again, we are reminded of St. Augustine, who said, "Let me know myself Lord, and I will know You" (Robb, 1983, p. 26). St. Teresa of Avila says, "Self-knowledge is not just a necessary foundation for holiness, but an integral part of God's gradual self-revelation to us" (Robb, 1983, p. 26). And again, "Those who seek truth seek God, whether they realize it or not" (Edith Stein, as cited in Beauregard & O'Leary, 2007).

The truth of God is the profound knowing that we are loved, that we are lovable. This knowing is more than a cognitive understanding, more than a belief; it's an affective knowing, an emotionally laden experience of knowing in every part of our being. Knowing that we are loved in this sense changes us. We become transformed. We realize that our needs can only be fulfilled by and through the One who first loved us—by the One who makes us so lovable.

The great spiritual writers all say the same thing. We should never flee from the self-knowledge that we continually make mistakes. We continually lack the love and acceptance and compassion that we so long for. It's only by passing through this knowledge that we find peace. God is not at the other side; God is in the mess. God is with us before, during, and after.

St. Ignatius of Loyola, one of the greatest spiritual guides of all time, talks about self-knowledge as the conflict between opposites: "light and darkness, freedom and unfreedom, life and death" (Robb, 1983, p. 21). This isn't unlike Carl Jung's principle of opposites. Jung believed that the human psyche is driven toward individuation by the energy created through the principle of opposites: the yin and the yang, the anima and the animus within each of us, the libido and thanatos energies. Jung believed that, like the polar opposites of a magnet, these energies propel us forward in our development and maturation. He believed that ultimately we move toward individuation, a state of being we were created to achieve.

Individuation, for Jung, was the ultimate experience of who we *are*, not of what we *do*. Being at peace with who you are absolutely requires self-knowledge and acceptance of both the darkness and the light and, as Jung points out, it is in this unification of opposites, the reconciling of all that is good with all that we deem less good, that we find our peace. The ultimate good, then, leads us outward and inward simultaneously. Knowing our own truth leads us to knowing others, which in turn leads us to knowing God. Teilhard de Chardin writes in *The Divine Milieu*:

> We must try to penetrate our most secret self, and examine our being from all sides. Let us try, patiently, to perceive the ocean of forces to which we are subjected and in which our growth is, as it were, steeped… And so, for the first time in my life perhaps (although I am supposed to meditate every day!), I took the lamp and, leaving the zone of everyday occupations and relationships where everything seems clear, I went down into my inmost self, to the deep abyss whence I feel dimly that my power of action emanates. But as I moved further and further away from the conventional certainties by which social life is superficially illuminated,

> I became aware that I was losing contact with myself. At each step of the descent a new person was disclosed within me of whose name I was no longer sure, and who no longer obeyed me. And when I had to stop my exploration because the path faded from beneath my steps, I found a bottomless abyss at my feet... At that moment... I felt the distress characteristic of a particle adrift in the universe, the distress which makes human wills founder daily under the crushing number of living things and stars. And if someone saved me, it was hearing the voice of the Gospel... speaking to me from the depth of the night: *ego sum noli timere* (It is I, be not afraid). (de Chardin, 1965)

As Robb (1983) says of this passage, the parts of himself that he didn't know are the parts that need healing, the parts that we often judge as unworthy and are denied. Our true selves can only be found when we come to know and accept all that we are. When we choose to live more than the mundane, we choose to "meet our inner selves on the journey" (Robb, 1983, p. 23). We meet these various parts of ourselves in many forms: in emotions, in dreams, in our imagination, in our confrontations at work and at home, in our pain, in our disappointments, and in our joys.

We meet ourselves in life, in life that is reflective and intentional, not in judging ourselves based on external laws and expectations. Robb emphasizes the difference between self-knowledge and knowing about yourself through objective measures, like psychological tests or other people reflecting back to you who they think you are. Self-knowledge is the kind of affective knowledge that moves you to a place within that's sacred and close to the Divine.

Again, Robb (1983) reminds us that this kind of inward journey isn't embarked on alone. Ironically, we need others in order to find our inner being. We need to surround ourselves with like-minded people. We need friends to share the journey. We need mentors who have walked this path before. We need to live life to the fullest, reflecting on our experiences and living our relationships in order to touch our centre.

So, where do we turn to for mentors? Mentoring used to be thought of as coming from the older, more experienced wise one providing a model for the younger, searching apprentice. In fact, a mentor can be of any age. What is valued and respected moves respectfully back and forth between the young and the old. Mentoring is a role of wisdom and inspiration; even a six-year-old can be inspiring.

We're moving into a new existence where men and women of all ages need each other. We have moved from a hierarchical model to an egalitarian model of community. We no longer expect that those in authority will be our guides. We've been disillusioned and disappointed too many times to blindly trust authority. Our guides are those whom we learn to trust and respect, not from their position in society, but from the way they live their lives. *"You will know them by their fruits"* Matthew 7:16 (NRSV). We learn to trust the wisdom and insights that come from a community of like-minded people. We learn to recognize the value of a person in *being*, and not in *doing*.

It's always a challenge to foster relationships that share deep, honest, and open feelings. But there's an increasing sense that we need each other more than ever before, a sense that competitiveness and separation from a supportive network fractures our ability to learn from one another and feel the value and worth of what we can add to the whole. The fragmentation and individualization of our culture necessitates that we adopt a mutuality model of working as a whole, interdependent group. This is a challenge to the old hierarchical model that for centuries was considered the norm and status quo. In God's plan of development, we need all aspects of the human person to be whole, fulfilled, and able to experience the peace and true joy life has to offer. We need to appreciate each individual, young and old, male and female, for one's contribution to each other's value in what is now a very small global community.

The challenge of fostering these nurturing relationships is that society sanctions success in very different terms. Society uses artificial perfection and materialism as its guide, thus producing expectations at every turn. These expectations then create a measurement of accountability to strive toward. This striving traps us in a mentality of trying to succeed according to what we can produce (*doing*) rather than who we become (*being*). Is it any wonder we neglect to foster meaningful relationships and mentorship? Relationships are about being, not about doing.

A spontaneous open response to life and relationship with God and others is always more life-fulfilling than what we can acquire or the things we produce. The simplicity of life is worth enjoying. We can experience a time and place where we feel safe and vulnerable enough to share our deep feelings, but it takes time and we need more practice at it. For some, this type of relationship is more typically ascribed to women, but many men, lots of them, are willing and strive to live the interior life. Fewer are willing to talk openly about their desires, because society is busy with the artificial trophies of more power, more money, more success, more virility, more technology, more, more, more.

We need renewed traditions to capture our sense of awe, our sense of beauty, and our sense of God. We need renewed efficacy of the Word, of truth, of life. We need to rekindle the sacredness of ritual and discipline. We need to renew our symbols and rituals in order to celebrate life and rites of passage. We need a new mosaic of different cultures, of sexual equality.

We need an inclusive notion that moves us all to a quiet love and acceptance of everyone.

Traditionally, we have often relegated matters of faith and spirituality to the clergy, but each of us is invited and capable of developing our own relationship with our God. God speaks to human nature at a deep level and gives us a message that we can understand personally. We just need to learn how to listen. We must have confidence that we always know what is true. Even when we question the validity of our own choices, when we know how to listen we hear deep in our gut what's true for each of us. We need to learn to trust these intuitions, these urgings of the Holy Spirit, to guide us. Let Holy solitude be your teacher.

> *I pray that your love will keep growing more and more, together with true knowledge and perfect judgement so that you will be able to choose what is best.* (Philippians 1:9–10, TEV)

We need to calm our psyche, to balk at the busyness of our world and the fast-paced bytes of the information super-highway. We need to find harmony in nature and with all creation. We can learn from the cultures that celebrate their oneness with nature and what she offers. Spending time in nature is the surest way to oneness, peace, and harmony. We need to balance what we take into ourselves and what we give back to Mother Earth. We have a responsibility to give back to the earth that which we take. It's in this balance that we find harmony in all creation.

MOTHER EARTH

I was there when my skies were blue
When my rivers were clear
When my forests rang with song.

I was there when you drew your first breath
When you took your first drink
I watched in disbelief as you turned
The sky to yellow
The rivers to brown
Drove the creatures small and large
Out of my forests.
I was there as you gasped your last breath
As you laid on the ground
Your knees pulled into your chest.

I was there as time heated the
Earth
Rivers made clear
Forests once again rang with song.

I was there but you were gone.
Gone forever…

(Ray Drost)

The universe works by its own rules. God has given nature her own free will. In Christ everything is inclusive, every person and all creation. When we approach nature with awe and respect, we approach the Creator. It is good to re-create, to nurture our being in the naked, untouched innocence of nature.

The timeless existentialist Rollo May, in *Man's Search for Himself*, claims that people who have lost their sense of identity also tend to lose their connection with nature—with the trees, the mountains, the animals, the birds. They lose the awe of a sunset and the majesty of the ocean. Anxiety tends to make us numb to nature; we withdraw from nature and lose our childlike spirit of adventure and discovery. May claims that inward feelings of emptiness are often paralleled by experiencing nature as empty, dried up, and dead.

Looking at the artists of the Renaissance, we can see the rebirth of nature in the works of Giotto. Giotto painted the natural form for the sake of its own beauty, unlike the stilted works of the Middle Ages, showing that when a human being experiences life in all its beauty and promise, he or she also experiences a lively connection to nature (May, 1953).

May also draws our attention to the Renaissance's renewed appreciation of the human body. Among many, we particularly see this in the powerful and magnificent works of Michelangelo. The Renaissance was a time of particular fervour for developing new ideas and new promise, for rebirth in all life. We recently returned from a tour of Italy and were particularly enthralled with the Renaissance gardens at Trivoli, which showcased not only the natural form and beauty of living plants, trees, and flowers, but also the flow of water in the many fountains and ponds.

A stroll through Claude Monet's gardens at Giverny, a hike through the Canadian Rockies, or a walk along the beaches of Maui cannot help but bring you closer to the awe of nature. The beauty of nature and art draws us beyond the mundane to nurture the human spirit within that is continually drawn to meaningfulness and transcendence.

I expand, I live;
stretch wings, release earth, swallow sky.
All things in my April morning
rise, lift, exalt.

Come to my morning.
I need you here with me
in this newborn day.
Come out of our long night
and be freshness, morning's joy.
Hand stretching to hand.
Eyes glistening.
Be.
Be so fully
that Powers and Thrones back away.

Release whatever holds you.
My morning needs you.
My world is hushed and waiting.
...Come.

(Mary Lynn Jones, 1982)

Awareness

chapter nine

We become spiritually rich when we discover the adventure within; when we are conscious of the oneness of all life; when we know the power of meditation; when we experience kinship with nature…

Only the wise man, only he whose thoughts are controlled and purified, makes the winds

> d the storms of the soul obey him… Today we are where our thoughts have taken us, and we are the architects—for better or worse—of our futures. (Allen, edited 1968, pp. 11–12)

We are called to be mystics, to be saints, to examine in a deeper way our own journey and exceed the usual limits of life's mundane existence. We can read about the lives of the saints, the sacred writings of mystics in the Christian tradition, but the challenge is to strive to be saintly in our everyday lives. Spirituality is a major component of life. To neglect the spiritual side of our existence is to neglect the opportunity to see beauty and purpose in all life, to transcend the ordinary, everyday experience of life and experience true joy in the midst of the ordinary. "In short, mysticism opens up a new layer of life" (Johnston, 1982, p. 38).

> In the search for me, I discovered Truth.
> In search for Truth, I discovered Love.
> In the search for Love, I discovered God.
> And in God, I found everything.
> (Author Unknown)

People don't know how to meditate. Our culture isn't conducive to nurturing the spiritual life. But, as Dyer (1998) so aptly illustrates, this is not only a contemporary problem:

Learn to be silent.
Let your
quiet mind
listen and absorb
(Pythagoras, 580 BC–500 BC)

All man's miseries derive from not being
Able to sit quietly in a room alone.
(Blaise Pascal, 1623–1662)

Hoffman (2005) criticizes the modernistic approach to studying about God. Psychology and theology alone have the tendency to intellectualize God. Knowing God, even in our limited, finite state, necessitates that we nurture our spirituality and faith with a human experience of God. The God concept and God image need to be nurtured together. These developmental processes are never stagnant. They must be fluid, experiential, rational, and yet always incomplete. This is humility. Finite created beings can never fully know the infinite Divine and Ultimate Being.

St. Thomas Aquinas, a thirteenth-century philosopher and theologian, spent most of his adult life writing numerous great works that are still studied and pondered to this day. His greatest work, the *Summa Theologica*, took him more than five years to complete. Such a great thinker who spent his entire life defending the Christian faith was humbled in

God. Some say it happened while he was Mass, and others speculate that he was sitting in front of the fireplace to keep warm on a damp winter's eve. Whenever it occurred, Thomas had a personal encounter with God. It's written that he experienced God in a personal way. After this momentous event, this great thinker claimed that all he had done to that point was like straw.

In order to nurture our own, personal experience of God, we have to constantly be aware of the spiritual side of our created being. Each of us has, within us, the calmness of God's Being, the Holy Spirit. We need to be in constant communication with this Spirit of God. In this union with the real live person of God, we must be present to each other in every minute of our existence. Sometimes people ask, "How do I pray? How do I know God exists?" The answer is to stay focused on Jesus' words and works. Look at Jesus' behaviour as a starting point. Jesus' behaviour demonstrates how a person is to respond to life. Look at Jesus' prayer, worship, meditation, and spiritual direction. He was never motivated to put on a show, prove his divinity, or judge others for their wrongdoings.

Constant communication must be part of our regular activities in order to develop and nurture an ongoing relationship with our God. In his prayer, Jesus called God Abba/Imma (Daddy/Mommy). Jesus shows us how to relate to God. It is through prayer that we develop a personal relationship with God. It is through prayer that we experience God and thus reconcile our rational God concept with our relational God image. If we want to know someone, and be in relationship, we must spend time together. When we love someone, we want to get to know that person and enjoy his or her company. This, then, becomes our priority.

> *But whenever you pray, go into your room and shut the door and pray to your Father who is in secret; and your Father who sees in secret will reward you. "When you are praying, do not heap up empty phrases as the Gentiles do; for they think that they will be heard because of their many words. Do not be like them, for your Father knows what you need before you ask him.* (Matthew 6:6–8, NRSV)

How do we know Jesus? We communicate daily. We pray the Scriptures. Why do we pray with Scripture? Because Scripture, more than any other source of learning, ultimately sheds the most light on our basic human questions. Scripture is the first measure, norm, guide, and light of our faith. Its importance comes from the fact that it expresses the faith of the first Christians close to Jesus, close to knowing God, and our knowledge and awareness of Jesus and God has grown since then. How we understand the Scriptures, the Word of God, unfolds as our journey progresses. Words, especially the Holy Word, create perceptions and perceptions create behaviours. Jesus of the Second Testament presents us with a loving God and a personal invitation to a lifetime journey of love and freedom. The Holy Word brings us to an understanding of our loving God.

> *For God so loved the world…* (John 3:16, NRSV)

A literal interpretation of religious scriptures can sometimes get us lost in the First Testament theologies of reward and punishment, of unequal grace or human manipulation of God's actions for those who beg for Divine intervention.

How then do we know the truth of Scripture? Always interpret Jesus' words through the lens of love. Jesus' words and works are always consistent. Pray with the Holy Word, for it is rightfully called the Living Word. God's Word will draw us beyond intellectual debates of what Scripture might mean to the affective truth of what love means. Use an easy translation that's written in plain language. The Bible is not a history book. The Christian Bible was written with the same truth that was there even before it was written, for truth is more than just an historical moment. Read the paragraphs, the verses that stir some movement within, and stay with that line for as long as it inspires you.

Any spiritual writing from holy men and women throughout history can be approached this way. The Holy Spirit moves you to the verses that are important for you, now. Scripture is the Living Word because God didn't die after the last book was written. God continues to inspire and speak to us through this Living Word and will continue to do so to the end of time. It contains everything we need for salvation but cannot be taken literally; it is developmental, showing the people of God getting to know and interpreting their God more clearly through time. The people of the Scriptures' relationship with God changed and grew collectively and personally. They moved toward salvation just as we are moving toward salvation, and salvation simply means accepting the love of God.

So, when are you going to have time for this? You might say, "I barely have time to cut the grass, do my laundry, and take my kids to the park. How will I find time to sit and read spiritual books?" These are real questions for real people. The answer is in our attitude toward our inward journey. We can approach all our daily routine tasks with the stance of gratitude in knowing that God is all-present, *omnipresent*—that is, constantly encountered. This attitude already puts us in the Presence, in the present. We experience closeness with God in many different ways out of our response to accepting God's love for us. We are all created unique, thus God communicates with each of us in our own special way.

When we care for and look after ourselves, we make space in our lives for a balance of connectedness with our God and the world around us. The word Sabbath means rest. It is good to rest from your daily duties and routines; it is good to spend time alone; it is good to enjoy the rhythm of life. God is in the wind, the air we breathe, *pneuma*—that is, Spirit. It isn't hard to find God if we're open to God's love. We don't fall in love unless we're drawn to something that attracts us. God is always extending a hand to us in caring friendship and love.

> *No one can come to me unless drawn by the Father who sent me.* (John 6:44, NRSV)

There are many stories to demonstrate the presence and goodness of God in our lives.

A big developer was building a multimillion-dollar project. There was a lot of activity around the site, with scores of men and machinery. The job site was almost totally congested when a double tandem trailer dump truck got stuck. The project manager moved in a large CAT dozer from another part of the site to pull the truck out. While the pull was taking place, the big chain they were pulling with broke, its pieces scattering over the men standing around. No one got hurt!

Then there was the time when a smaller crane was lifting the weights to set up a larger crane. A couple of huge weights fell from the crane-lift while men were standing around. No one got hurt!

A man was up on a ladder, some fifteen feet high, when the ladder slipped. The fellow below wasn't strong enough to hold up the ladder long enough for the man on top to get down, but he still managed to hold on for an unusually long period of time… where did his strength come from?

A man once told Frank about how he was given spiritual directives and insights throughout the day when talking to people. These thoughts seemed to be given to him out of the blue, and when he shared them with whomever he was speaking with at the time, they were always received well and seemed to be just what the person needed to hear at that moment.

How about the young boy, about twelve years old, who leaned over a bridge railing? He was surveying the situation for fishing. While looking down, talking to his friends, he fell over the railing, hurtling some twenty feet down. He fell not in the water, but onto the shallow shore on top of his bicycle paddle. He never got hurt, only stunned!

Frank's dad once told him of an experience of how tangible God can be in prayer. He was accustomed to saying the rosary on his way to work every morning, a forty-five-minute drive to a meat-packing plant in Kitchener. He would religiously say the last decade of the rosary for the "poor souls in purgatory" (purgatory, being the place we are all expected to go in order to be purified before entering heaven). The belief was that this time of purification could be shortened if your faithful friends on earth prayed for you. One morning, he was startled by a clear voice: "Stop praying for us; pray for your family." The focus of his prayer changed from that moment on.

These stories have all been shared with us, each pointing to a personal awareness of God's constant presence in our daily, routine existence. Some might say these are ordinary stories of luck or coincidence. What makes them stories of faith? They were told by men of faith, men who have a personal relationship with their God, men who experienced these events as the presence of God in their lives. We meet God in the extraordinary moments of our ordinary lives.

We adapt to the person we're in relationship with. Our God is a God of unconditional love, constantly there for us, showing us how to live and how to love. Unconditional love is a real thing that only touches us at a moment here and a moment there. We can speculate about its effects, but most often it is incomprehensible. There may be occasions when we get a glimpse of this type of acceptance within our human experience, but actually meditating and reflecting on the reality of an unconditionally loving God is scary because it's so unfamiliar to us. To face love dead on, for what that actually means, calls each one of us to a very beautiful place. Consequently, we begin to realize that the only answer to the pain and suffering of the world is through the love Jesus showed us. To experience this for even a moment is a transformation we must taste. It hurts to be in love. It hurts to love to this extent.

Therefore, real meaning in life can only be found in our moments, moments with our God, Jesus, and moments with those we are intimate with and share ourselves with. If we care about God or another person, we must share ourselves with them. These moments, appreciating the harmony of the beautiful gifts of nature and life around us, seeing the beauty in all God's creation, bring us glimpses that tell us we have finally arrived. We have finally arrived at the place of peace and harmony—even if only for a moment.

In prayer, always be open to God in the surprise; in the quiet, calm, contemplative moments of our prayer; in the awestruck moments of an experience of nature; or in a most intimate sharing of two people's sacredness. It is here that we find God and experience prayer, by not knowing where our imagination or reality leaves off and the providence of God's Spirit takes over.

Spiritual matters are most often non-cognitive. It hurts to love, and love is all about being present to life. Spend time with Jesus and you'll be at peace, for there is no peace without prayer.

> This holy exercise of prayer… is more essential for a Christian who wants to live a Christian life than is the earth which supports us, the air which we breathe, the bread which

> sustains us and the heart which beats in our breast necessary to us for human life. (John Eudes, trans. 1989)

Prayer is the only thing that saves us from self-deceit and self-dishonesty. Prayer allows for self-correction. Prayer brings us toward harmony and wholeness. Sin corrects itself with prayer. Separation from one's centre cannot stand the uniting force of prayer, but a broken and fragmented spirit, detached from self, produces much pain for that person and anyone around him or her. The good news is that God loves us in spite of ourselves and that we are saved and can rest easy in spite of our weaknesses. God doesn't judge, but loves us into wholeness. Thus, through the Divine presence of God we embrace love, faith, and hope.

> *[God] does not deal with us according to our sins, nor repay us according to our iniquities. For as the heavens are high above the earth, so great is his steadfast love toward those who fear [love] him; as far as the east is from the west, so far he removes our transgressions from us. As a father [mother] has compassion for his [her] children, so the Lord has compassion for those who fear [love] him. For [God] knows how we were made.* (Psalm 103:10–14, NRSV)

The power to transform comes from the tremendous love of Jesus, a power to establish peace in our lives. Jesus' transformative love touches all aspects of our being: body, mind, spirit, and actions. We need to nourish our bodies with healthy food and exercise. We need to nourish our minds with reflective readings. We need to nourish our spirits with meditation for peace of mind and clarity. We need to share our lives with good people, especially those on a spiritual journey. We need to relax in the moments, the safe gift of the *now.* We need to let go. We don't need to experience it all. The absolute all is in nothing. Freedom.

In the Dalai Lama's *The Fullness of Emptiness* (1986), he writes about the importance of practicing awareness. He says that practicing awareness of the present moment helps us to recognize the emptiness in being attached to worldly and material pleasures. According to the Dalai Lama, we become attached to that which we believe we need before we have the awareness of what we need. He says that attachment comes before recognition. To strive to experience more of everything is really to achieve nothing. To let go of everything is to acquire all. What in us must be left behind if Jesus is to become the centre of our lives?

LOVE ONE ANOTHER AS I HAVE LOVED *You*

chapter ten

For you were called to freedom, brothers and sisters; only do not use your freedom as an opportunity for self-indulgence, but through love become salves to one another… Live by the Spirit… the fruit of the Spirit is love, joy, peace, patience, kindness, generosity, faithfulness, gentleness, and

> *self-control… If you sow to your own flesh, you will reap corruption from the flesh; but if you sow to the Spirit, you will reap eternal life from the Spirit.* (Galatians 5:13, 16, 22–23; 6:8, NRSV)

We need to believe and receive our new freedom of love and acceptance from God. A whole new life is available to us through simplicity and prayer. We have to believe we can *become*, and that's where life has its value. What goes around comes around; we reap what we sow. We know and have seen the actions of nature and of God. Generosity and sharing life always spurs more generosity and sharing of life. If we want the world and others to operate out of more goodness toward all, we have to start with ourselves operating out of more goodness toward all. We need to be more Christ-like.

We aren't aware of how special we can be. The most important way to show we care is to share ourselves, for it truly is in giving that we receive. It's only when we open our hearts to others that we receive the strength to continue on our journey inward. Only in accepting God's unconditional love, then turning around and giving that love to others, can we receive in our hearts our reward of utmost joy. When we perform acts of the Spirit, we are filled with the Spirit.

Only the promise of something fantastic would motivate a person to embark, and continue, on this inward journey. In our postmodern society, people often don't know what, or who, they can believe. The inward journey isn't about believing or trusting others; it's about believing and trusting in your own goodness and giftedness, which will lead you to believing and trusting in others and ultimately in God.

Although this may at first glance seem egotistical, it's anything but self-centred. We are made of this world but in the image and likeness of our Creator. We can trust that God loves us and will always love us, regardless of what we think or do. The unconditional love of God for us sheds light on how to read the daily events of our lives. It tells us that all that's good is from God and all that isn't good comes from either our finitude as creations or our selfishness—that is, our sins. As finite creations, we experience floods, droughts, sickness, death, pain, and suffering of various magnitudes. Our selfishness brings suffering to ourselves and others because of our greed and self-centeredness.

If God can raise the dead, as shown in Jesus' resurrection, certainly God can draw life for us out of the dreadful moments of our sufferings, which don't come from anything Divine. What pleases God when we suffer isn't our suffering, but our persevering trust and faith in continuing Love, in spite of what it appears to be. What pleases God when we suffer is our courageous effort to overcome the sources of suffering and oppression. God, as the most loving parent, doesn't send suffering but rather "cries with us" when we suffer, says Fuellenbach (2000) in *Throw Fire*. And as one of the traditional prayers and hymns of the church asks, "Who is this God who gets hurt when we get hurt?" In our suffering, God is present, giving us strength, endurance, and hope by telling us that suffering isn't the last word of our life story; life, joy, peace and resurrection are the exciting last words.

> *[God] will wipe every tear from their eyes. Death will be no more; mourning and crying and pain will be no more, for the first things have passed away.* (Revelation 21:4, NRSV)

This passage shows the gentleness and faithfulness of our gracious God. God is with us eternally. We become like the God we worship, so be a humble and gentle instrument of God's love. In choosing to live with acceptance, gratitude, and compassion, we experience fullness of life. The deepest joys of life will depend on our image of God, on whether our God is a God of total love, or a God who at times is a God of love and at other times a God of wrath.

At a human level, a psychological level, we create a judgmental God because we cannot accept our own behaviours. We believe we are sinful and need a lot of purification and correction to be pure and perfect enough for any pure and perfect image of God we can conjure up. However, that image of God does us no good. We fail, and our image of God fails along with us.

The Second Testament, in Jesus, shows us the Christian God of unconditional love and compassion. Jesus had a choice. Jesus chose to return into Jerusalem *to show us* his great love and mission. Jesus' sole purpose in becoming human was to show us God's overwhelming unconditional love for us. He died out of love. He was driven by his passion to show how much God loves us. He knew he was going to die.

People were killed in three main ways in those times: being stoned, being thrown off a cliff, or being crucified. The message wasn't about death and suffering; it was about unconditional, passionate love. Consider Jesus' behaviour with the woman at the well, who was married six times. Were there any judgments or condemnations? Never. He just told her to go back to town and tell them what she had experienced while she was with him. What do you think she experienced? Love and acceptance—something completely contrary to the culture of the time!

Jesus is always first to show that the pain of sin is separation from one's self and others and God: lack of wholeness, lack of oneness, a separation from one's own person and sacredness. Jesus always tried to show God's love as a response, as though to say, "If you look at me, you see God." But God never takes away our intellect and free will. We can choose our image of God. This choice will deeply condition how we experience God and how we respond to others. To know the God you worship is to understand who you are becoming.

In the late Pope John Paul II's General Audience to the faithful, he is quoted for his understanding of hell. Hell is the "self-imposed" punishment of those who choose to refuse God's love and mercy. "God is infinitely good." "Eternal damnation is never the initiative of God." Hell is not a sign of God's anger, but an indication of human free will. We must be careful interpreting the biblical descriptions of hell, which are metaphorical (John Paul II, 1999). Hell is possible because we can refuse the love of God. But hell is not probable, because God will search for every last one of us.

Even the apostles got it wrong at first. They lived with Jesus and still missed his obvious message of love. This is vindicated in Luke's gospel in the three parables of God's mercy.

> *Now all the tax collectors and sinners were coming near to listen to [Jesus]. And the Pharisees and the scribes were grumbling and saying, "This fellow welcomes sinners and eats with them." So he told them this parable.* (Luke 15:1–3, NRSV)

Luke continues with Jesus telling the stories of the lost sheep, the lost drachma, and the lost son.

Jesus never condemns, but always searches for those separated from love.

> *For I am convinced that neither death, nor life, nor angels, nor rulers, nor things present, nor things to come, nor powers, nor height, nor depth, nor anything else in all creation, will be able to separate us from the love of God in Christ Jesus our Lord.* (Romans 8:38–39, NRSV)

In 1983, Brother Roger Schulz, the founder of an all-inclusive ecumenical prayer community in Taizé, a tiny village in France, addressed the World Council of Churches assembly in Vancouver. This humble man of prayer said, "God does not want us to be dragged down with guilt, but filled with trust and forgiveness. God is never a tormentor of the human conscience" (as cited by Argan, 2005). This world-famous contemplative community is open to all religions, promoting non-violence, justice, and peace. Brother Rogers' words show us that Taizé's all-inclusive spirituality isn't an escape from the world; rather, it engages the world through prayer.

We're all responsible for our own journey. We're free to take what we need for life from a deep, loving, interior, unconditional friendship with our God. We necessarily hold all of life together for its good. Karl Rahner, a world-renowned German theologian, confirms that we need to observe all human activities of unrest by holding everything together from a position of rest. What we become in our own holiness, our travels through life, depends on our ability to offer responses of love to all we meet.

What is your story? As a young man? As a young woman? As a middle-aged man? As a middle-aged woman? As an elderly man? As an elderly woman? What is your gospel story? How has God been working in your life since the beginning of your journey here on earth? And what is unfolding in your future relationship with God? Is your relationship one of peace and joy and closeness with God? Are you moving toward oneness or are you becoming more fragmented, fragile, and lost in the sea of noise, glamour, busyness, and struggles of life? What overwhelms you from trusting God?

Don't stay trapped. Make choices toward becoming whole, human, and free. We can reconcile our own emotional fragmentation and heal our souls. There is so much beauty around us: the arts, the classics, music, nature, the innocence of children, and the camaraderie of good friends. Absorb the awe of life and the spiritual experiences that life offers us.

We need each other. Find God. Find a trusting spiritual companion. Find someone. Pray that God will bring someone into your life for support and care. The only response to all the pain and suffering in the world is love. It's the only response that makes sense and works. Look at Jesus. He will show you the way. God is necessarily always abundantly generous. Do Not Worry.

> *[Jesus] said to his disciples, "Therefore I tell you, do not worry about your life, what you will eat, or about your body, what you will wear. For life is more than food, and the body more than clothing. Consider the ravens: they neither sow nor reap, they have neither storehouse nor barn, and yet God feeds them. Of how much more value are you than the birds! And can any of you by worrying add a single hour to your span of life? If then you are not able to do so small a thing as that, why do you worry about the rest? Consider the lilies, how they grow: they neither toil nor spin; yet I tell you, even Solomon in all his glory was not clothed like one of these. But if God so clothes the grass of the field, which is alive today and tomorrow is thrown into the oven, how much more will he clothe you—you of little faith! And do not keep striving for what you are to eat and what you are to drink, and do not keep worrying. For it is the nations of the world that strive after all these things, and your Father [Mother] knows that you need them. Instead strive for his kingdom [God; Abba/Imma], and these things will be given to you as well. Do not be afraid, little flock, for it is your Father's [Mother's] good pleasure to give you the kingdom [what your heart desires].*

here your treasure is, there your heart will lso." (Luke 12:22–32, 34, NRSV)

Our journey through life won't be without some pain and suffering, but with the spiritual support of an intimate companion like Jesus—our God—it will definitely be a lot less painful and anxiety-ridden than being alone and living without support or hope. A life lived on the surface and with record speed, filled with noise and activity, will unfortunately cause us to become unaware of life altogether.

But, as it is written,

> *"What no eye has seen, nor ear heard, nor the human heart conceived, what God has prepared for those who love him"—these things God has revealed to us through the Spirit; for the Spirit searches everything, even the depths of God. For what human being knows what is truly human except the human spirit that is within? So also no one comprehends what is truly God's except the Spirit of God. Now we have received not the spirit of the world, but the Spirit that is from God, so that we may understand the gifts bestowed on us by God. And we speak of these things in words not taught by human wisdom but taught by the Spirit, interpreting spiritual things to those who are spiritual.* (1 Corinthians 2:9–13, NRSV)

We can feel the transcendence of God in only if we feel safe with God. We are not called to be perfect but to walk with God in our imperfection, secure in knowing this is all God desires for us. Our downfall is to hide from God rather than to accept the invitation, which is simply to walk with our Father/Mother God. Don't just change to another set of rules, looking to legalize boundaries that contain us and give us God in a shallow little package. Just respond to God in openness, inclusively and totally.

> *When you are praying, do not heap up empty phrases as the Gentiles do; for they think that they will be heard because of their many words. Do not be like them, for your Father knows what you need before you ask him.* (Matthew 6:7–8, NRSV)

We will never find those things which we keep trying so desperately to run to. What's out there doesn't make us happy; it doesn't give us life. The journey inward is subjective. It's about our own human person, often alone and misunderstood, but alone and at peace and joy with ourselves and ultimately finding our Holy Spirit within. What's in our thoughts? Where do they lead our bodies?

> *For where your treasure is, there your heart will be also.* (Matthew 6:21, NRSV)

Dear friends, fullness of life is about knowing and being aware of the movements of your Spirit—that is, knowing how God speaks to you. What moves you? Saint Ignatius Loyola, a Spanish Jesuit who was inspired by the providence of God to learn the active movements of one's spirit toward or away from God, formally called this *discernment of the spirits.* Our inward spirit experiences consolation, the state of being consoled and comforted, or desolation, the action of desolation, grief, sadness, loneliness, devastation, and ruin. Always be aware of how you are leading yourself. If you can, always make decisions during times of consolation.

Be comfortable with yourself. Be at peace in your aloneness. Be friends with the quiet. Love nature and beautiful things, for here you will find the presence of God. Look at all things as an opportunity to see the transcendence of life. Our ordinary, everyday lives show us constant symbols of the transcendent life, because life is good. When you're in touch with your heart, the heart of life, peace will be with you.

Experiences of humanity are seldom of ecstasy. The real lifelong experience of ecstasy comes from living a life of transcendence and mystical insightfulness. This awareness isn't a high, but can be part of making one's ordinary life even better. God created everything good. A God of all goodness, wholeness, and oneness can only create good. Being connected to a very deep spiritual place makes sense of the whole journey and all our experiences. We must start from within, then go out. Look at the life of Jesus as an example.

Our closing hope is that you really believe in the love and guidance of a relationship with Jesus. And in the words of a traditional blessing often used by Frank's mentor, Ubald Duchesneau:

May you hear God's voice
in your heart,
Know His touch in
your life,
And feel His love
each day.
(Author Unknown)

At first it's like trying to fall in love with something intangible, seeing and hearing and feeling nothing. At first it doesn't seem real. Of course Jesus is real and is speaking to us all the time, but we simply can't see or hear him at first—not until we learn to recognize the speech of Jesus, the activity and behaviours of God. Then we laugh and say, "Wow, God is real and does speak! I just didn't hear before."

Don't miss the opportunity to taste an experience of life with the spiritual, a deep interior experience of life, a connection with what's real, what's lasting. Only connecting with your deepest spiritual sense tells you who you truly are. You are a gift to behold.

What keeps us from God? Nothing. We live in a culture that doesn't support deep, quiet spiritual development. We don't live in caves or monasteries, as some of the early saints did. We live in a fast-paced, technology-based world where people work fourteen hours a day or more in cycles of mass activity and noise. But please believe and trust our history, the history that shows us how to live as the saints did, the history that shows us there are ordinary men and women today who do live a sacred and holy existence—as Jesus did. These are modern-day mystics who we can emulate. Trust the sacredness of ritual and discipline. Create a new journey for yourself with your God, a fantastic relationship that will never let you down. Create this relationship, however you can, by:

- Remembering you are made in the image and likeness of God.
- Being alone.
- Being quiet.
- Having your own prayer space, both in formal and informal places.
- Having a spiritual friend or two.
- Not worrying, instead letting God look after your troubles.
- Enjoying the beauty of the music, food, wine, and nature around you.
- Loving, playing, praying, and working.

- Taking care of yourself (Frank's dad's last words to him).
- Having fun, without getting into trouble (Dorothy's dad's last words to her).

And speaking of last words, don't forget Jesus' last words to us:

> *Peace I leave with you; my peace I give to you.* (John 14:27, NRSV)

references

Allen, J. (1968). *As a man thinketh.* Edited for Contemporary readers by W. R. Webb. Kansas City, MO: Hallmark.

Argan, G. (2005, August 29). May Br. Roger's peace live on. *Western Catholic Reporter.* Retrieved from http://wcr.ab.ca/old-site/columns/editorials/2005/editorial082905.shtml

Avery, T. (2008, May 31). One in four don't believe in God: Poll finds. *The Canadian Press.* Retrieved from http://www.thestar.com/News/Canada/article/434725.

Bandura, A. (1977). *Social learning theory.* Englewood Cliffs, NJ: Prentice-Hall.

Beauregard, M. & O'Leary, D. (2007). *The spiritual brain: A neuroscientist's case for the existence of the soul.* New York, NY: Harper Collins and Harper One.

Bianchi, E. C. (1988). Jungian psychology and religious experience. In R. L. Moore (Ed.), *Carl Jung and Christian spirituality* (pp. 16–37). New York, NY: Paulist Press.

Bourke, V. J. (1964). *The pocket Aquinas: Selections from the writings of St. Thomas*. New York, NY: Washington Square Press.

Corveleyn, J., & Luyten, P. (2005). Psychodynamic psychologies and religion. In R. F. Paloutzian & C. L. Park (Eds.), *Handbook of the psychology of religion and spirituality* (pp. 80–100). New York, NY: Guilford Press.

Cox, R. H. (2005). A proposed paradigm for the developmental stages of spirituality. In R. H. Cox, B. Ervin-Cox, & L. Hoffman (Eds.), *Spirituality and psychological health* (pp. 33–56). Colorado Springs, CO: Colorado School of Professional Psychology Press.

Dalai Lama, The (1986). The fullness of emptiness. In *Leaning on the Moment: Interviews from Parabola* (pp. 231–249). New York, NY: Parabola Books.

De Chardin, T. s.j. (1965). *The Divine milieu*. New York, NY: Harper Torchbooks.

Dyer, W. W. (1998). *Wisdom of the ages: 60 days to enlightenment.* New York, NY: Harper Collins.

Emmon, R. A. (1999). *The psychology of ultimate concerns: Motivation and spirituality in personality.* New York, NY: Guilford Press.

Erikson, E. (1968). *Identity, youth and crisis.* New York, NY: W.W. Norton.

Eudes, J. (1989). *The fourth foundation of Christian life and holiness: Prayer*. (L. M. Glendon, Trans.). In W. M. Thompson (Ed.), *Bérulle and the French school: Selected writings* (pp. 313–314. Mahwah, NJ: Paulist Press.

Feeney, J. A. (1999). *Adult romantic attachment and couple relationships.* In J. Cassidy & P. R. Shaver (Eds.), *Handbook of attachment: Theory, research, and clinical applications* (pp. 355–377). New York, NY: Guilford Press.

Fowler, J. (1981). *Stages of faith.* San Francisco, CA: Harper and Row.

Fowler, J. W. (1996). Pluralism and oneness in religious experience: William James, faith development theory, and clinical practice. In E. P. Shafranske (Ed.), *Religion and the clinical practice of psychology.* Washington, DC: American Psychological Association.

Fuellenbach, J. s.v.d. (2000) *Throw fire.* (2nd ed.). Indore, India: Satprakashan Sanchar Kendra.

Hoffman, L. (2005). A developmental perspective on the God image. In R. H. Cox, B. Ervin-Cox, & L. Hoffman (Eds.), *Spirituality and psychological health* (pp. 129–147). Colorado Springs, CO: Colorado School of Professional Psychology Press.

Hood, R. W. (1977). Differential triggering of mystical experience as a function of self actualization. *Review of Religious Research, 18,* 264–270.

John Paul II. (1999, July 28). General audience. Retrieved from http://www.vatican.va/holy_father/john_paul_ii/audiences/1999/documents/hf_jp-ii_aud_28071999_en.html

Johnston, W. (1982). *The inner eye of love: Mysticism and religion.* New York, NY: Harper & Row.

Jones, M. L. (1982). *What a sunrise!* [Sherwood Park, AB: Informal publication]. Copy in possession of author.

Kirkpatrick, L. A. (1998). God as substitute attachment figure: A longitudinal study of adult attachment style and religious change in college students. *Personality and Social Psychology Bulletin, 24,* 961–973.

May, R. (1967). *Man's search for himself.* Bergenfield, NJ: New American Library. (Original work published in 1953).

Nierenberg, B., & Sheldon, A. (2005). Spirituality and children. In R. H. Cox, B. Ervin-Cox, & L. Hoffman (Eds.), *Spirituality and psychological health* (pp. 57–74). Colorado Springs, CO: Colorado School of Professional Psychology Press.

Noffke, J. L., & Hall, T. W. (2007). Attachment psychotherapy and God image. *Journal of Spirituality in Mental Health, 9,* 57–78.

Oser, F. (1991). The development of religious judgment. In F. K. Oser & W. G. Scarlett (Eds.). *Religious development in childhood and adolescence* (pp. 5–26). San Francisco, CA: Jossey-Bass.

Oser, F., & Gmünder, P. (1991). *Religious judgment: A developmental perspective.* Birmingham, AL: Religious Education Press.

Pargament, K. I., Magyar-Russell, G. M., & Murray-Swank, N. A. (2005). The sacred and the search for significance: Religion as a unique process. *Journal of Social Issues, 61,* 665–687.

Parker, S. (2006.) Measuring faith development. *Journal of Psychology and Theology, 34,* 337–348.

Piaget, J. (1970). Piaget's theory. In P. H. Mussen (Ed.), *Carmichael's manual of child psychology, 3rd ed., Vol. 1* (pp. 703–732). New York, NY: John Wiley and Sons.

Piedmont, R. L. (2005) The role of personality in understanding religious and spiritual constructs. In R. F. Paloutzian & C. L. Park (Eds.), *Handbook of the psychology of religion and spirituality* (pp. 253–273). New York, NY: Guilford Press.

Reber, A. S., & Reber, E. (1995). *The penguin dictionary of psychology (3rd ed.).* London, UK: Penguin Books.

Rizzuto, A.-M. (1979). *The birth of the living God: A psychoanalytic study.* Chicago, IL: University of Chicago Press.

Robb, P. s.j. (1983). *Conversion as a human experience.* Institute for Spiritual Leadership, Chicago, IL.

Rodgers, R. (1964). Something good. [Recorded by Julie Andrews and Christopher Plummer]. On *The sound of music: Soundtrack album.* [Record]. New York, NY: RCA Victor.

Simpson, J. A. (1999). Attachment theory in modern evolutionary perspective. In J. Cassidy & P. R. Shaver (Eds.), *Handbook of attachment: Theory, research, and clinical applications* (pp. 115–140). New York, NY: Guilford Press.

Thalbourne, M. A. (2003). *A glossary of terms used in parapsychology* (2nd ed.). Charlottesville, VA: Puente.

Webster's ninth new collegiate dictionary. (1984). Springfield, MA: Merriam-Webster.

Weinfield, N. S., Sroufe, L. A., Egeland, B., & Carlson, E. A. (1999). *The nature of individual differences in infant-caregiver attachment.* In J. Cassidy & P. R. Shaver (Eds.), *Handbook of attachment: Theory, research, and clinical applications* (pp. 68–88). New York, NY: Guilford Press.

Zinnbauer, B. J., & Pargament, K. I. (2005). Religiousness and spirituality. In R. F. Paloutzian & C. L. Park (Eds.). *Handbook of the psychology of religion and spirituality* (pp. 21–42). New York, NY: Guilford Press.